EDITOR IN CHIEF®

Book C1 Grammar Disasters and Punctuation Faux Pas

SERIES TITLES:

Editor in Chief® A1 • Editor in Chief® B1 • Editor in Chief® C1

Editor in Chief® A2 • Editor in Chief® B2 • Editor in Chief® C2

Created by Michael Baker

Written by Cheryl Block, Linda Borla,
Gaeir Dietrich & Margaret Hockett

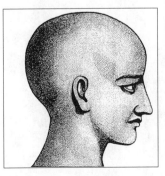

© 1999
THE CRITICAL THINKING CO.
(BRIGHT MINDS™)
www.CriticalThinking.com
P.O. Box 1610 • Seaside • CA 93955-1610
Phone 800-458-4849 • FAX 831-393-3277
ISBN 0-89455-517-0
Printed in the United States of America

Illustration by Kate Simon Huntley

English consultant: Marc F. Bertonasco, Ph.D.
Professor of English
California State University Sacramento

TABLE OF CONTENTS

TO THE TEACHER

Objective

Editor in Chief® reinforces the rules of written English by providing the student with practice in editing a variety of formats. Students develop a basic understanding of the rules of grammar and mechanics in context and exercise their critical thinking abilities by identifying content errors. Book A covers the skills generally taught in grades 4–6, Book B covers those taught in grades 6–8, and Book C covers skills for grades 8 and up.

Rationale

The key difference between *Editor in Chief*® and most grammar series is the focus on editing in context. The grammatical and mechanical errors inserted into the activities are based on general instructional guidelines for specific grade levels; the content level, however, remains ungraded, allowing usage of these materials at many instructional levels. Styles and content are varied to sustain interest and broaden the student's exposure to different writing formats such as letters, directions, schedules, and dialogue. The illustrations integrated into the context of the activities further spark student interest. The editing skills developed can be applied to the student's own writing.

Activity

Each activity consists of 1–4 content errors (discrepancy between the illustration/caption and the writing sample) and 9–15 errors in spelling, mechanics, and grammar. The student is asked to identify these errors and make the appropriate corrections. An editing checklist, included on page viii of this book, may be used by the student to aid in the editing task. Most corrections involve the insertion, modification, or deletion of punctuation marks, capitals, and single words and short phrases within the text. Some corrections will involve rewriting of single sentences or repositioning of sentences within a paragraph. Each writing sample is based on an accompanying illustration and caption. Information in the illustration and caption is correct. (A content error occurs only where the story is contradicted by the illustration or caption.) The student may insert corrections and recopy the corrected article. Activities are sequenced according to the type, number, and level of errors included and the complexity of the subject matter.

Using the Answer Key

The answer key on page 35 lists corrections for each article. Each numbered error correction is followed by a shorthand explanation of the error type (more information on specific rules can be found in the Grammar Guide on page 75). The teacher may choose to provide students with the number and type of errors prior to editing. In some instances, a student may be able to correct an error in more than one way. The answer key gives some obvious choices, but the teacher may choose to accept other answers that make sense and are grammatically and mechanically correct.

Teaching Suggestions

Editor in Chief® can be used as an individual or group activity for instruction, reinforcement, practice, and assessment of English grammar and mechanics. When introducing a new rule, a teacher can use one article as an instructional example and a second as an assessment of students' independent understanding. This book provides an excellent tool for authentic assessment of students' knowledge of grammar and mechanics. The Scope and Sequence on page viii gives teachers an overview of the types of errors included in each article, enabling them to individualize lessons more easily.

Suggested Uses for *Editor in Chief*®

Regular Usage

- Group instruction—EIC format is ideal for overhead projector.

- Cooperative Learning—Students edit and exchange work to proofread.

- Homework—Individual activities can follow class instruction.

Extension Activities

- Students write their own paragraphs for editing.

- EIC fosters class discussion of writing errors and how to avoid them.

- Checklist can be used to transfer editing skills to other writing activities.

Sources and Standards

In preparing this manuscript, we used the following references as standards for spelling, grammar, punctuation, and usage:

The American Heritage Dictionary, 3rd ed. (Boston: Houghton Mifflin Company, 1993).

The Chicago Manual of Style, 14th ed. (Chicago: The University of Chicago Press, 1993).

The Merriam-Webster Concise Handbook for Writers (Springfield, Mass.: Merriam-Webster Inc, 1991).

The Merriam-Webster Dictionary of English Usage (Springfield, Mass.: Merriam-Webster Inc, 1989).

The New York Public Library Writer's Guide to Style and Usage (New York: HarperCollins Publishers, Inc., 1994).

Warriner's English Grammar and Composition: Complete Course, Liberty Edition (Orlando: Harcourt Brace Jovanovich, 1986).

SCOPE AND SEQUENCE: EDITOR IN CHIEF® BOOK C1

TYPE OF ERROR	Exercise Number 1–33
GRAMMAR/USAGE	
Adjective/adverb	2, 5, 9, 11, 26, 29
Agreement	2, 3, 4, 5, 6, 7, 9, 10, 11, 13, 14, 16, 17, 19, 20, 21, 23, 24, 25, 27, 29, 31
Article: a or an	4, 31
Conjunction: correlat.	8, 21, 22
Dangling modifier	14, 17, 18, 19, 26, 33
Misplaced modifier	9, 13, 18, 26, 29
Nominative case	12, 32
Parallel structure	2, 9, 10, 19, 21
Pronoun: ambiguous	11, 14, 15, 19, 24, 29, 31
Pronoun: with as/than	6, 15
Pronoun: subj./object	3, 6, 11, 16, 17, 21, 24, 31
Pronoun: reflexive	31
Subjunctive mood	15, 20, 25, 26
Tense: simple	5, 7, 8, 11, 24, 26, 31
Tense: perfect	3, 6, 11, 22, 23, 26
Unnecessary words	6, 30
Verbals	6, 14, 20, 24, 32, 33
Verb: infinitive	2, 9, 10, 14
Verb: participle	3, 6, 7, 11
Word pair (confused)	3, 8, 12, 15, 24
SPELLING	2, 5, 6, 7, 9, 11, 14, 15, 16, 17, 19, 21, 23, 26, 29, 33
PUNCTUATION	
Apostrophe	1, 4, 7, 16, 18, 19, 21, 24, 26, 30, 31
Colon	11, 12, 14, 18, 21, 27, 31
Comma: absolute	16, 25
Comma: ambiguity	24, 31, 32
Comma: appositive	2, 5, 13, 31
Comma: conjunction	1, 2, 8, 13, 19, 22, 26
Comma: contrast	4, 17, 28
Comma: coord. adjec.	1, 13, 18, 23, 31, 32
Comma: date/address	3, 8, 10, 24, 27
Comma: dependent	3, 7, 18, 19, 21, 26
Comma: dialogue	6, 7, 22, 26
Comma: interrupter	29
Comma: intro/transit.	7, 13, 14, 17, 18, 26, 28, 30, 33
Comma: letter	10, 19, 26
Comma: nonessent.	1, 4, 5, 11, 13, 14, 16, 26, 29
Comma: quotation	1, 3, 6, 18, 19, 26
Comma: series	10, 33
Comma: splice	1, 13, 26
Comma: unnecessary	1, 2, 3, 4, 8, 11, 13, 14, 16, 17, 19, 20, 22, 26, 28
Exclamation point	23, 29, 30
Hyphen	8, 14, 18, 26
Multiple punctuation	12, 20, 21
Parentheses	2, 8, 18, 21, 24, 25, 28, 30, 32
Period	1, 2, 3, 8, 10, 21, 24, 27, 28, 32, 33
Semicolon	3, 7, 11, 13, 16, 21, 24, 28, 30
Sentence fragment	2, 12, 16, 24, 33
Question mark	7, 13, 20, 29
Quotation marks	1, 3, 6, 7, 9, 14, 16, 18, 21, 28, 29, 33
CAPITALIZATION	
Compass direction	23, 31
Proper noun/adjective	1, 4, 7, 9, 12, 15, 20
Title/abbreviation	6, 8, 12, 30
Quotations	6, 26, 31
Seasons, holidays	7, 23, 32

STYLES AND TOPICS: EDITOR IN CHIEF® BOOK C1

EXERCISE TITLE	WRITING STYLE	CONTENT: TOPIC	Fiction/ Nonfiction
1. American First Ladies	expository/descriptive	Amer. History: first ladies	nonfiction
2. History of the Dome	expository/descriptive	Architecture: dome	nonfiction
3. An Inspirational Pitch	narrative	Biography/Sports: Jim Abbott	nonfiction
4. Flight of Fantasy	expository/descriptive	Science: flight	nonfiction
5. Pirate Spiders	descriptive	Biology: spiders	nonfiction
6. On His Toes	narrative	Mystery: detective	fiction
7. Lightning Strikes Out	narrative (dialogue)	Sports: horse racing	fiction
8. Setting Sail	descriptive (brochure)	Education: sailing class	fiction
9. The Money Tree	narrative	Student outing: discovery	fiction
10. On Shaky Ground	descriptive (letter)	Natural disaster: earthquake	fiction
11. A Nobel Endeavor	expository/descriptive	Sci/Biography: explosives	nonfiction
12. Diamond in the "Ruff"	descriptive	Hobby: dog shows	fiction
13. A Horse of a Different Color	expository/descriptive	Biology: sea horse	nonfiction
14. Animal Partnerships	expository	Biology: symbiosis	nonfiction
15. A Sound Environment	narrative/expository	Science: sound waves	nonfiction
16. A Contest of Wills	narrative	Ethnic pride: parade	fiction
17. Virtually Real	descriptive	Sci/Technology: virtual reality	nonfiction
18. A Unique Mammal	expository/descriptive	Biology: platypus	nonfiction
19. It's a Zoo Out There	persuasive (letter)	Career: job application	fiction
20. A for Ama	narrative	Geography: Kenya	fiction
21. Something Old, Something New	expository/descriptive	Environment: recycling	nonfiction
22. All Washed Up	narrative	Adventure: flood	fiction
23. Recipe for Destruction	expository/description	Science: tornadoes	nonfiction
24. Placid Thrills	narrative	Winter sports: Lake Placid	fiction
25. Stalk Your Claim	narrative	Writing: book signing	fiction
26. Double Take	narrative	Adventure: movie filming	fiction
27. Granting Health	persuasive (letter)	Medicine: research grant	fiction
28. It's Never Too Late	expository	Exercise: seniors	nonfiction
29. Drawing on Psychology	expository	Psychology/Art: perception	nonfiction
30. On Track	narrative	Hobby: model trains	fiction
31. Scheduled for Success	narrative (schedule)	Time management: schedule	fiction
32. An Honest Fake	narrative	Social club: initiation	fiction
33. Moore Money	descriptive	Economics: personal finance	fiction

Editor in Chief® — Editing Checklist

CAPITALIZATION

Are the correct words capitalized? Do other words need capitals?

CONTENT

Does the information in the paragraph match the caption and illustration?

GRAMMAR & USAGE

Agreement:

Does the verb agree with the subject? Is the subject collective? Does the pronoun agree with the noun or pronoun it replaces? Does the adjective agree with the noun or pronoun it modifies?

Correlative conjunctions:

Are either/or and neither/nor used correctly?

Dangling modifier:

Does the grammatical subject of the sentence immediately follow the introductory phrase, or does the sentence need to be rewritten?

Misplaced modifier:

Does the modifier make sense where it is placed within the sentence?

Parallel structure:

Are parallel ideas written in the same grammatical form within a sentence?

Pronoun:

Is it used as a subject or an object? Is the correct form used? Is it in the right place? Is it clear to which noun the pronoun refers?

Verbals:

Is the correct verb form used as a noun, adjective, or adverb?

Verb tense:

Is the correct form used for both helping verb and participle? Is the correct form used for both main verb and other verbs?

Usage:

Is the correct word used? Does a word need to be changed?

Word pairs that are easily confused:

Is the correct word used?

PUNCTUATION

Apostrophe:

Is the word a contraction? Is the word a plural or possessive? Is the apostrophe in the right place?

Colon:

Is it used correctly? Is it placed correctly?

Comma:

Is it needed to separate words, dates, phrases, or clauses? Is it placed correctly?

Exclamation point:

Is it used correctly?

Hyphen:

Is it used correctly in compound numbers or unit modifiers?

Question mark:

Is the sentence or quotation a question? Is the question mark placed correctly?

Quotation marks:

Is each part of the divided quotation enclosed? Are other punctuation marks placed correctly inside or outside the quotation marks? Are song, story, or chapter titles enclosed? Are single quotation marks required?

Run-on sentence:

Should this be more than one sentence? Should a period, a semicolon, or a conjunction be used?

Semicolon:

Is it needed? Is it used correctly?

Sentence fragment:

Is this a complete sentence?

SPELLING

Are the words spelled correctly? Is the plural form correct?

PROOFREADING

Should punctuation be inserted or deleted? Are there too many punctuation marks? Are parentheses used correctly in pairs? Are articles used correctly?

1. American First Ladies

Presidential first ladies have been an active force in American politics for about 300 years. These womens' roles have been many, and varied In 1800, Abigail Adams, dubbed "Mrs. President", was a fervent activist against antifederalists. Sarah Polk served as President James Polk's chief aide during his term in the 1830s. As an outspoken abolitionist, Mary Lincoln had an enormous influence on President Lincoln's policies.

Eleanor Roosevelt remembered as one of the most publicly active first ladies, worked in support of the New Deal and integration and was the first of the first ladies to testify before Congress, she was particularly famous for her worldwide humanitarian work and was elected to chair the United Nation's Human Rights Commission in 1946 helping to draft the Universal Declaration of Human Rights.

Rosalynn Carter was Jimmy's political partner during his term from 1977 to 1981. She supervised the Commission on

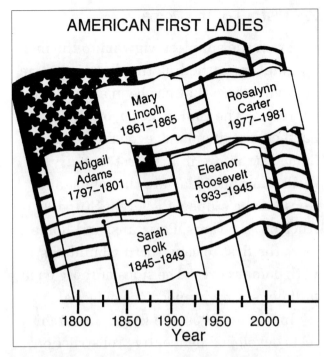

Presidential first ladies have been actively involved in American politics since the earliest years of the republic.

Mental Health and helped to draft the Mental Health Systems Act of 1980.

Presidential wives have been playing an active vital role throughout American political history. In the future, perhaps all presidential spouses will continue to do so.

Find the 11 errors in this activity.
There are no errors in the illustration or the caption.

---

2. History of the Dome

From the simplest wigwam to the more magnificent cathedral, the dome is a form of architecture that has been around for centuries. The Indian stupa, originally an earthen burial mound, evolved into a domed structure in the First Century B.C. (Still standing today are the tallest and finest of the stupas, the Great Stupa.) Ancient Assyrians, Parisians, and Romans were the first to constructing buildings with dome rooves. The sides of those early buildings were rounded or polygonal.

In the A.D. 500s, the Byzantine architects developed pendentive construction, providing a dynamic solution to the problem of setting a round dome. Atop a square or rectangular building. The top dome rests upon a larger dome from which the top and four corner segments have been removed (see diagram.) The Hagia Sophia, built in Constantinople between 532 and 537 B.C., is one of the supreme achievements in world architecture and it offers a prime example of pendentive construction. Light flows through forty

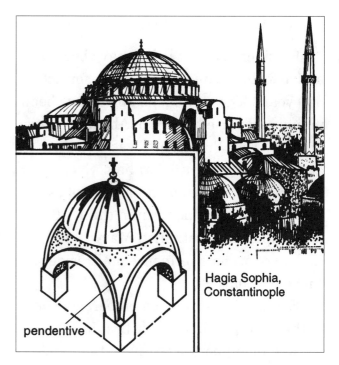

pendentive

Hagia Sophia,
Constantinople

Dome roofs were first built in the ancient civilizations of Assyria, Persia, and Rome. In the A.D. 500s, the Byzantines developed pendentive construction, which placed a small dome on a larger dome from which the rim segments had been removed. The Hagia Sophia, a cathedral built by the Byzantines, is an excellent example of pendentive dome construction.

windows, that encircle the base of the dome, giving the illusion that the dome is suspended in space.

Find the 12 errors in this activity.
There are no errors in the illustration or the caption.

---

3. An Inspirational Pitch

There are many outstanding athletes in every sport, but few has been able to overcome a handicap and succeed to the degree that Jim Abbott has; he epitomizes the word "hero". Jim was born on Sept. 19, 1967 with only one hand, yet he has managed to win a gold medal in baseball at the 1988 Winter Olympics and become a major league pitcher for the California Angels and the New York Mets.

Jim was fitted with a prosthetic hand at age five but found it awkward and stopped using it by age six. He has never wore an artificial limb since. Instead, his father devised a technique, now known as the "Abbott switch", that enabled Jim to field the ball without using any artificial device. While he throws the ball with his left hand, he balances his glove on his right wrist; on the follow-through, he slips his hand into the glove to field the ball, after catching a ball, he tucks the glove under his right arm, rolls the ball down his left arm, and throws. Perfecting this technique, required hours of practice for his dad and he. He is now so accomplished at these maneuvers, that people watching

Jim Abbott, one-handed pitcher for the Yankees and the Angels, has had a career that included a Golden Spikes Award for outstanding amateur baseball player in the United States and a gold medal in the August 1988 Olympics.

him for the first time don't realize he is one-armed.

For Jim, the high point in his career was the no-hitter he pitched in September, 1993 against the Cleveland Indians. It embodied Jim's philosophy: "I don't go out there to be courageous or inspirational. I go out there to get hitters out."

Find the 13 errors in this activity.
There are no errors in the illustration or the caption.

---

4. Flight of Fantasy

"He maneuvered his small jetstar into a crevice below the edge of the canyon. He hoped to avoid being seen by the patrol ships circling overhead in the vivid Nebulean sky, he knew he will be unable to last long in a fight. Suddenly, they spotted him. He thrust his craft into high speed and dove into the canyon, hoping to outmaneuver if not outrun his pursuers. The small ship banked sharply from side to side, dodging speeding missiles and jutting rocks. Squeezing the ship through a narrow opening among two rocks, he barely managed to escape the larger patrol ship following them."

As exciting as the above scenario seems, it is not possible outside of the movies. Some spacecraft, such as the space shuttle, are designed to fly like airplanes in Earths atmosphere, but they would not be able to fly this way in the vacuum of open space. In order to bank (tilt laterally and inwardly in flight), a spaceship would require air to create lift on the wings; it could not bank in outer space because space lacks the air pressure needed for lift. It would also be difficult for a actual spaceship to make sudden changes in direction; changed direction,

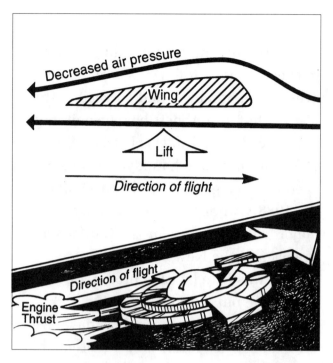

In Earth's atmosphere, air pressure creates lift on the wings of an airplane, allowing it to maneuver more easily. Outer space lacks the air pressure needed to create lift; spacecraft must rely on engine thrust to change directions.

a spaceship relies on the thrust created by rocket engines. The pilot first has to shut down the rocket engines, that are pushing the spaceship in one direction, he then ignites a set of rockets located on the same side from the direction in which he wants to go. This lack of maneuverability would make for very slow-paced action scenes if the movies were true-to-life.

**Find the 11 errors in this activity.
There are no errors in the illustration or the caption.**

5. Pirate Spiders

The group of arachnids known as cannibal spiders, or pirate spiders feed on other spiders. They belong to the family Mitosis. About a dozen mimetid species live in the United States. The Black Widow spider is not included among them.

Many of these spiders is small, about a quarter of an inch or more in length. Their bodies are delicately marked with dark lines and spots. The front pairs of legs have a series of long and short spines that the spider uses to grasp its victim firmly.

The pirate spider moves slow and stealthily to captured it's prey. It enters the web of another spider and pulls on a line of the web. The unknowing spider, who will have hurry anxiously to the spot in anticipation of a good meal, is caught by surprise. The pirate attacks it, injecting a poisonous venom that paralyzes its victim and then slowly sucks the juices from the body of the unlucky spider.

Pirate spiders, or cannibal spiders, belong to the family Mimetidae. There are about a dozen mimetid species in the United States, including the black widow. The mimetids
• Are a quarter of an inch or less in length
• Usually do not spin webs
• Often take over the webs of other spiders
• Are slow moving and stealthy
• Have spines on the front pairs of legs
• Are venomous
• Eat other spiders

Find the 13 errors in this activity.
There are no errors in the illustration or the caption.

6. On His Toes

Detective Novak had finally solved a rash of apartment house burglaries that had been plaguing the area for months. "How were you able to crack this case Detective?" asked the reporter.

"We have had a possible suspect for months, but he had always managed to elude us, leaving no obvious evidence behind. Him and me were waging a personal battle, but he was not as smart as me. I knew he will get careless. I was finally able to retrace his steps", said the Detective. "From his shoes. Both had clues on its toes."

The detective then proceeded to explain his strategy to the reporter.

"As I was questioning the suspect, I noticed a small drop of pizza sauce on the tip of his left shoe. A pizza delivery boy had recall that as he was arriving to deliver a pizza on the evening of the burglary, he collided with a man rushing out of the apartment building."

"But how did you place the suspect inside the burglarized apartment"?

"Our suspect uses a unique brand of foot powder that is sold only in one local

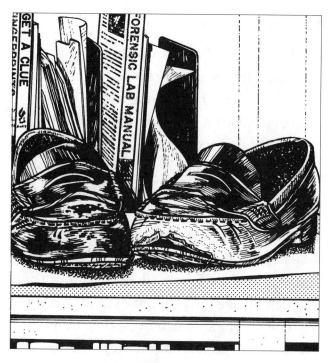

Detective Novak had noticed what appeared to be a small drop of pizza sauce on the tip of one of the suspect's shoes; the suspect's other shoe was separating at the toe. The shoes were sent to the lab for analysis.

shop. The soul of his right shoe is separated at the toe, and some of his foot powder dribbled onto the carpeting. I was able to remove a small amount of powder and match it to the residue in his shoe."

"I guess a good detective always has to think on his feet," the reporter observed wryly.

Find the 14 errors in this activity.
There are no errors in the illustration or the caption.

---

7. Lightning Strikes Out

"We have beautiful Fall weather for today's state fair charity race featuring an outstanding array of horses. The horses are starting to get in position, some is already lined up at the gate.

"There off! Greenoak Fields White Lightning is in the lead with George Kantor's Fancy Free close on his heels. As they round the corner Fancy Free tries to take the lead. It's Fancy Free and White Lightning. Coming up on the outside is Fleet Feet from Oakdale Stables, battling with Quickstep.

"This is a close race folks. Fleet Feet surges ahead of Quickstep and is trying to overtake the leaders. The question is Would she be able to catch up. Fancy Free and White Lightning are neck and tail. Look out! White Lightning has stumbled; the crowd are stunned. His riders still on, but the delay has cost him the race. Fleet Feet and Fancy Free are crossing the line, second and first. What a loss for White Lightning.

Fancy Free, from George Kantor's stables, and White Lightning, from Greenoak Fields, are neck and neck when White Lightning stumbles. Fleet Feet and Fancy Free come in first and second, respectively, in the race.

Find the 15 errors in this activity.
There are no errors in the illustration or the caption.

8. Setting Sail

Classes: Fridays from 4:00 P.M to 6:00 P.M., weather permitting

Prerequisite: Either completion of beginning sailing or an equivalent course

Location: Shoreline Park on Surf Blvd. Seattle

Wear appropriate clothing, and rubber soled shoes or boating shoes. Life jackets will been provided. Registration is on September 10.

Complete the form below, listing all previous experience in sailing or boating. Proof of completion of the Beginning Sailing class (or an equivalent course, will be required at the first class.

Jim Turner wants to take Treehill College's new advanced sailing class this fall; he has filled out the registration form as required.

Name: _James Turner_   SSN: _000-00-000_

Address: _645 Via Nueva Avenue, Apt. 3_   Phone: _(206) 555-0029_

Bellevue, Wash 98006   Age—_17_

Years of sailing experience: _6 mo.s_

Type of experience: _I sailed a 14-foot catamaran in Hawaii and completed the beginning sailing class next summer._

List the name and phone number of the person we should contact in an emergency.

Name: _Mrs. Martha Turner_   Phone: _(206) 555-8893_

Parental permission is required for students under 18.

James Turner has my permission to enroll in the advanced sailing class, therefore, he can participate in all course activities.

Martha Turner
Parent/Guardian

Find the 13 errors in this activity.
There are no errors in the illustration or the caption.

---

9. The Money Tree

Some high school students involved in the city's 7th annual park restoration and cleanup day this weekend did cleanup in a real big way! The students uncovered a paper bag while planting a tree filled with money. The police, who took charge when the bag was found, believes the money was stolen in a bank robbery twelve years ago. The culprits were caught, but never was the money found.

The students who recovered the treasure, nearly $5,000, are hoping the bank will offer them a reward for there honesty. "I've never seen so much money in my life," said one of the young men, but I certainly wouldn't have any problem thinking of ways to spending it. Who says money doesn't grow on trees? he added. Bank Officers were not available for comment.

During the city's park restoration and cleanup day, students from Blach High School uncovered a plastic bag containing $50,000. Police theorize that the money was stolen from a bank twenty years ago.

Find the 13 errors in this activity.
There are no errors in the illustration or the caption.

---

10. On Shaky Ground

157 Faultline Drive
Golden Fields CA 95091
October 24, 1989

Dear Gina

I know that you have been worried about us since the earthquake. Were all fine, although still a little shaken up.

There was alot of damage downtown. Buildings collapsed, and many fires breaked out because of the broken gas lines. Tragically, several people were killed by falling rocks.

When the earthquake hit, I was in San Jose and couldn't get home for hours. Many freeways were closed because of structural damage, collapsing overpasses, or rocks that had slid; as a result, I had to drive home along back roads. The next morning I heard that after I have driven home, the bridge I had crossed was de-clared unsafe!

My parents house was a disaster area! Closets spilled their contents shelves jettisoned dishes, hutches fell on their faces, and glass shards hurtled every-where!

My Dad said that everything were moving so much that he couldn't even get

Jose wrote to his friend Gina from his home in Green Meadows, where many old downtown buildings collapsed and other buildings were severely damaged. Falling bricks caused several deaths, and broken gas lines resulted in many fires. People in the city and surrounding areas were without running water and electricity for days.

out of his chair. I asked my mom if it was noisy with everything crashing to the floor and glass breaking. She said, "I was so scared that I didn't hear a thing".

Well, I have to go now. There's still alot of cleaning up to do!
Love
Jose

Find the 16 errors in this activity.
There are no errors in the illustration or the caption.

11. A Nobel Endeavor

It seems ironic that the inventor of one of the world's most destructive forces would ultimately be remembered. As the creator of one of the world's most endurable humanitarian legacies.

In the mid-18th century, nitroglycerin was the most common used explosive, however, nitroglycerin is highly volatile and can explode if jarred even slightly. A nitroglycerin explosion is triggered by a chemical chain reaction, that is impossible to stop once it has started.

In the 1860s, Swedish chemist Alfred Nobel owned a nitroglycerin factory. It was him who invented dynamite, an explosive that was safer because it could be handled more easy than nitroglycerin. To create dynamite, he mixed nitroglycerin with diatomite, a porous, earthlike substance. The resulting dry mixture of nitroglycerin and diatomite were more resistant to both shock and heat than was nitroglycerin alone.

Another of Nobel's inventions, the blasting cap, allowed for safer usage of it. An electric current detonated the blasting cap, which then detonated the dynamite. This latter invention made a fortune for

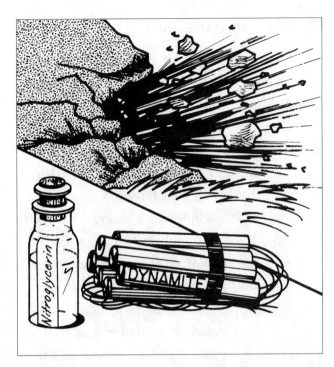

Alfred Nobel's inventions, dynamite and the blasting cap used to safely detonate the dynamite, replaced nitroglycerin, the explosive most commonly used in the mid-1800s. The success of Nobel's inventions enabled him to establish the world-renowned Nobel prizes.

Nobel; with this fortune, he established the Nobel prizes. These annual awards are given to persons worldwide whom have made significant contributions to the "good of humanity" in the following fields chemistry, physics, physiology/medicine, literature, international peace, and economic science.

Find the 12 errors in this activity.
There are no errors in the illustration or the caption.

---

12. Diamond in the "Ruff"

Diamond winner of Best in Show at the recent Newchester Kennel Club dog show is top dog. The five-year-old English Setter is owned and shown by Kathy Pruitt, Veterinarian, of Scarsdale. "This dog's a real jewel," said his ecstatic owner, "Diamond is this girl's best friend!".

You might wonder how a dog is judged to be the best in the show? First, each breed of dog is evaluated seperately by an uninterested judge. Judge is based on breed standards for: a dog's appearance, head and body structure, color and coat, temperament, and gait; the standards are approved by the American Kennel Club. The best of each breed then goes on to the group competition. Each breed belongs to a specific group. There are seven groups: sporting, hound, working, herding, terrier, and toy. The first-place dog from each breed competes for Best in Show.

Even at the final level of judging, the dogs are not compared to each other but are judged according to the standards of its particular breed. Therefore Best in

Diamond, a five-year-old English setter, took Best in Show (BIS) at the Newchester dog show. The Best in Show is selected from the first-place winners of each of the seven groups. Kathy Pruitt, D.V.M. hopes that Diamond's next litter will follow in their mom's famous footsteps.

Show is awarded to the dog that is considered the best representative of its breed. Often, subtle differences in overall showmanship become critical factors in selecting the best dog.

> **Find the 15 errors in this activity.**
> **There are no errors in the illustration or the caption.**

13. A Horse of a Different Color

The sea horse is unique in many ways. It coils its tail around plants and clings there while sucking up passing crustaceans through its pipettelike snout. It can swim weakly with its dorsal fin but usually floats along upright in the currents. The largest sea horse, *Hippocampus ingens*, can grow to 14 inches.

Certain species have also adapted their skin texture to match their environment, for example, *H. bargibanti,* the smallest sea horse, has bumps that mimic the texture of corral. As chameleons, many species of sea horses can change color to blend in with their background. The sea horse and the chameleon also shares the trait of dependent eye movement; this trait helps the sea horse ambushes its prey in the reefs and sea grass meadows.

Among fishes the male is often the nurture parent, caring for the eggs until they hatch. Male sea horses carry this behavior one step farther. The female sea horse deposits her eggs in the male's brood pouch. He then carrys the eggs until they hatch as completely independent, miniature sea horses.

A growing trade in sea horses, particu-

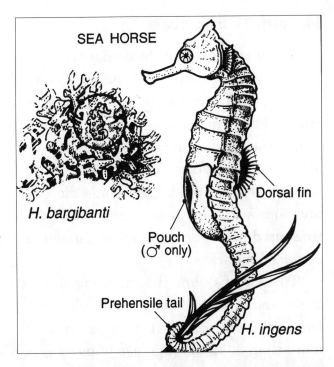

SEA HORSE

H. bargibanti

Dorsal fin

Pouch (♂ only)

Prehensile tail

H. ingens

The sea horse shares some common traits with the chameleon. Both have the ability to move each eye independently and to camouflage themselves by changing color. Some sea horses, such as *H. bargibanti*, the smallest sea horse, also use their skin texture as camouflage. Sea horses range in size from 3/4" to 14" long.

larly in Asia, has now endanger these special creatures. Used primarily in pharmaceuticals, the largest market for sea horses is mainland China. Dredging and pollution have also damaged many of the sea horses' coastal habitats.

Find the 13 errors in this activity.
There are no errors in the illustration or the caption.

14. Animal Partnerships

Many animals have formed a symbiotic relationship, or mutually beneficial partnership, with another species. The hermit crab's shell is not strong enough to stop a hungry octopus so the crab carries sea anemones on its back for protection. The octopus or other predators avoids the anemone's stinging tentacles. Protected from predators, the anemone is carried to new feeding areas.

The goby fish and the snapping shrimp live together as roommates and relies on one another for survival. There are no more than 30 kinds of gobies in partnerships with shrimp. The shrimp digs a nesting hole that provides both it and the goby with a ready made escape from enemies. In exchange, the shrimp relies on the goby, which sees better, to serve as lookout. The shrimp will rest one of its antennae on the goby; if a predator approaches, the goby would rapidly flick its tail signaling the shrimp to hide.

In the marine world, various kinds of fish and shrimp specialize in cleaning other sea creatures, a cleaner shrimp for instance will clean inside the mouth of a fish by removing bacteria, fungi, or tiny animals, caught in the fish's teeth. The remora hitchhikes rides on: sharks, rays, whales, and other sea creatures. Using a

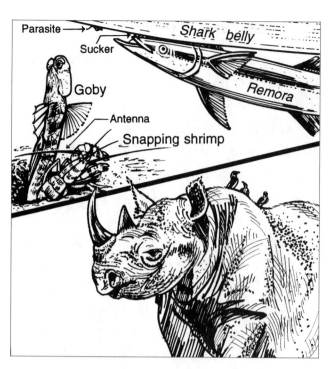

The snapping shrimp relies on its roommate, the goby fish, for protection; more than 30 kinds of gobies have partnerships with shrimp. The remora attaches itself to a host and gathers parasites and scraps; the rhinoceros bird feeds on insects that plague the rhinoceros.

sucker on top of its head, a remora attaches itself to a host. The remora benefits from the easy access to food, using its protruding jaw to collect both scraps dropped by its host and parasites it scrapes from the host's body.

Offering a similar service on land is several types of birds. The rhinoceros bird, for example, will perch on the back of the rhinoceros to eat the swarms of annoying insects that continually torment it.

Find the 14 errors in this activity.
There are no errors in the illustration or the caption.

---

15. A Sound Environment

Boom bah dah boom! I love studying to the beat of the latest tune, but as Mahmoud and me were doing our science lesson, my song was interrupted by the smoke alarm. (Can you believe it was set off by Dad's "cooking?") I again picked up the beat as we resumed our lesson on sound.

We read that sound is created when an object vibrates. When a tuning fork is struck, the prongs vibrate back and forth, pushing and pulling on the surrounding air and causing waves. By vibrating slowly, a large tuning fork makes sound waves of low *frequency*. Smaller tuning forks make sound waves of higher frequency because they vibrate more rapidly. Frequency is measured in cycles per second (cps).

"Whose playing the piano?" Mahmoud asked suddenly. My mom had hit the highest note having a frequency of 1500 cycles per second. Mahmoud could certainly hear it better than me (I had to strain!).

Next, we learned how sounds can differ in *amplitude*, or loudness. The distance the prongs of the tuning fork move back and forth determines amplitude. The affect of a small amount of movement is a quiet sound. The greater the distance the prongs move, the greater the displacement of air and the louder the sound. We com-

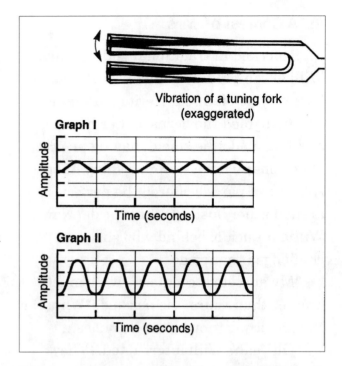

Vibration of a tuning fork (exaggerated)

Graph I

Amplitude / Time (seconds)

Graph II

Amplitude / Time (seconds)

The two students consulted the above graphs to compare amplitude (loudness): the greater the amplitude, the louder the sound. Below are some sample (approximate) frequency ranges.
- piano: 30–15,000 cps
- speech: 85–1100 cps

pared illustrations in our text. The two graphs showed tones of the same frequency; however, the wave in the second graph represented a quieter tone.

Far above, a jet broke the sound barrier. Vaguely aware of it, I thought, "If that sound was any softer, I wouldn't hear it at all." Mahmoud, however, was exasperated. "Who can study here?" he ranted. "If I would have known there would be so much noise, I would have studied sound at home, where it's quiet!" Was he inferring that my home was not?

Find the 12 errors in this activity.
There are no errors in the illustration or the caption.

---

16. A Contest of Wills

Bedecked in traditional viking armor. Willi Olson proudly guided her Morgan horse in the biannual Heritage Parade. She had glued the horns on her helmet and had made the shield, having an octet of peripheral circles, from a shiny hubcap. A heritage parade offered the perfect arena for her busting ethnic pride. Now William Lucido, behind who she rode, challenged that pride.

"My ancestors conquests were much greater than yours," he boasted. "Why, the Roman acquisitions were immense…"

"Oh yeah? Willi interrupted. "They weren't so great. The Vikings were super-lative seafarers! They reached north America long before Columbus…"

As the retorts flew, Willi leaned far-ther and farther toward her opponent her heavy weapon swinging precariously. Before she knew it, Willi has slid out of her saddle and was sprawling on the parade ground as a ragdoll. William laughed so hard that he fell out of his chariot. His fall, in turn, set off Willi's laughter.

"I guess neither of us have much to be

The planning committee selects just one winner of the costume contest in the yearly Heritage Parade. Sure of an award, Willi Olson rides proudly before arguing with William (riding ahead of her) and falling off her horse.

proud of now!" said William, wiping the dirt off his face. Soon, the two had made up and became friends.

"I guess the conquests of our ancestors aren't important," said Willi. "What really matter are the contributions we make ourselves." They applauded loudly as the planning committee announced their costume contest winners.

Find the 16 errors in this activity.
There are no errors in the illustration or the caption.

---

17. Virtually Real

"I'm slipping off the rock ledge. I-I don't think I can hold on anymore!" you shout as you grope wildly for a jutting stone—anything—that might prolong your tentative hold on the cliff's face. Up and down, runs the sheer rock wall to which you are plastered. You can hardly contain you're terror, because you are looking straight down into a mile-deep canyon. You've had enough. With shaking hands, your headgear tears off to find yourself in the security of your own living room.

The canyon "exists in the memory of a computer not in the real world. Virtual reality programs turn photographs of scenery into three-dimensional models, that you view through the tiny televisions in special headgear. Sound is also used to help simulate reality (distant "objects" are quieter than closer ones;) they are relayed through speakers located in the handgear. Wiring in special globes allow the computer to keep track of where you "are" in the virtual world and how you are "manipulating" any virtual objects. The computer creates a continuous presentation, which becomes the user's "world."

With a virtual reality program, a user could envision herself in the scene above. Sounds are piped into the headgear as she views a 3-D virtual world on tiny televisions. Wires running from the gloves to a computer provide constant feedback about hand movements.

Since they eliminate the danger associated with training situations, virtual reality programs have shown promise in medicine, aeronautics, and engineering. They can also help whomever uses them conquer the fear of high places!

Find the 13 errors in this activity.
There are no errors in the illustration or the caption.

---

18. A Unique Mammal

The platypus is one of only two egg laying mammals. (The other is the spiny anteater, or echidna.) The platypus is a monotreme, a mammalian order distinct from the marsupials and placentals.

The platypus inhibits a variety of waterways; streams, rivers, lakes, and ponds. It feeds primarily on small animals (shellfish, worms, insects and water plants that it finds, when it dives to the waters bottom. Unlike other mammals living in or near water, the platypus cannot dive for very long, it stays underwater for about an hour.

The platypus lives in a burrow near the water in a bank. The female digs the burrow, which may be up to 50 feet long, and makes a nest of moist leaves for her eggs. She lies from 1 to 3 eggs, which have soft leathery shells like those of reptiles. The female incubates the eggs until they hatch, about 10 days. During this time the female keeps the opening to the burrow plugged.

Newborn platypuses are hairy and about one inch long. Like all female mam-

Although the platypus has a ducklike bill and lays eggs, it is a true mammal, having hair (although the young are born hairless) and nursing its young. Platypuses live along waterways and can stay underwater for about 60 seconds while feeding on bottom-dwelling animals and plants.

mals, the mother platypus has mammary glands that secrete milk. Holding the tiny platypuses against her body with her tail, they nurse. It is several months before the young platypuses leave their burrow for the first time.

Find the 14 errors in this activity.
There are no errors in the illustration or the caption.

---

19. It's a Zoo Out There

410 View Street
Fayetteville, AR 72702
June 16, 1994

Adam B. Fujimoto Director
Cincinnati Zoo
3400 Vine Street
Cincinnati, OH 45220

Dear Mr. Fujimoto,

I wish to apply for the position of nursery vet tech advertised by your institution in the June 15 issue of the *Cincinnati Post*. Graduating in the top third of my class, two years' of training in animal health technology at the University of Cincinnati has been completed, and I am looking for a full-time position in animal care.

I admire the high caliber of the behavioral research conducted by your institution, and am familiar with several of your recent articles on animal behavior; "The Social Structure of the Prairie Dog Community," "The Effect of Captivity on Endangered Species", and "Communication for the Species." My four years experience as a pet-sitter, in which I was completely responsible for the care of a diverse population of animals, give me an excellent

Amanda submitted a copy of her resume when she applied for a position with the Cincinnati Zoo.

background for your current job opening. I work well with animals; there is a special bond among they and I.

I believe that I am a good match for your institution and would be very affective in this. I am creative, hard working, and have a lot of knowledge in many aspects of animal care. Please find enclosed a copy of my resume. Thank you for your consolation.

Sincerely
Amanda Doolittle
Amanda Doolittle

**Find the 17 errors in this activity.
There are no errors in the illustration or the caption.**

20. A for Ama

Ama is starting to panic. She wants all As in geography, and the semesters paper on Kenya is almost due! Born in America, Ama knows little about her ancestors' homeland; she appeals to Cousin Jomo, which is very familiar with the Kenyan territory. When she asks, "Kenya help me?," he gives her the following information:

- Many Kenyans speak the swahili language.
- The Prime Meridian divides Kenya so that it lies in both the Northern and Southern Hemispheres.
- Tourist attractions both include the sandy beaches of the coast and the inland animal reserves.
- On the exotic safaris, of whom we hear so much, hunters are allowed to shoot only with cameras.

Jomo hopes he has been of assistance. How else can he help her.

"What I really want to know is how it feels to be in Kenya?" Ama says dreamily. "I'm sure the morning sun is gorgeous as it rises over the South Atlantic Ocean!"

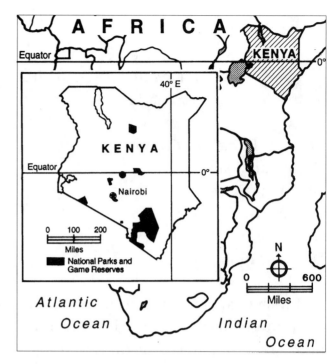

In order to complete her assignment, Ama is gathering information about the African country of Kenya.

"Well, if I was you," Jomo says, I'd go along with Aunt Jessie when she visits our relatives this month."

"I'd love to." says Ama, waking up to reality, "but in geography, I want to get an A for 'awesome;' if I were in Kenya, I'd get an F for 'far away.'"

**Find the 16 errors in this activity.
There are no errors in the illustration or the caption.**

---

21. Something Old, Something New

What really happens to the bottles and cans we recycle daily?. The technology of recycling has expand tremendously as scientists not only learn to remake the same products from old ones but also to create entirely new products. Used glass bottles can be melted down and turned into new bottles or into fiberglass insulation. Clear plastic bottles can be recycled into new bottles (not used for food), or it can end up as the stuffing in a sleeping bag (fiberfill!)

The three basic steps to recycling materials include: sorting the recyclable materials from the waste, processing the sorted materials into raw materials, and to make new products from these raw materials Recycling glass requires an additional step. The glass must be sorted by weight before it is processed, if colored and clear glass are melted together, they produce a muddy brown glass that most manafacturers find unacceptable for their products.

Once separated, magnets are used to remove any metal caps or lids. Then the glass is crushed, and paper labels are removed by suction. The resulting crushed glass, called cullet, is mixed with sand and melted in a glass furnace. The melted

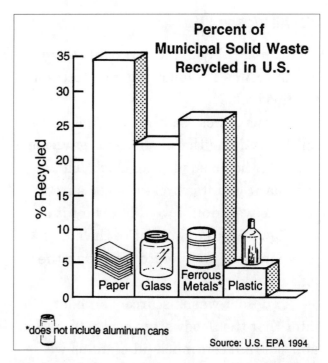

The above graph shows, for several types of materials, the percentage of the discarded material that is recycled. For example, 22% of all glass thrown away is recycled. Glass bottles require sorting by color prior to processing them for recycling.

glass can then be molded into new containers or spun into fiberglass insulation.

Glass is an excellent material for recycling, because, like metal, it can be melted down and reused over and over again. When we compare the proportions of materials that consumers recycle, glass ranks second; about 22% of the glass thrown away is recycled, compared to about 10% of plastic.

**Find the 15 errors in this activity.
There are no errors in the illustration or the caption.**

---

22. All Washed Up

At his Friday night liars' club, Gerald Smith recites the following anecdote about the flood of 89.

"It was almost bedtime for Amos and I, but I was doing the wash. Amos gave me a warning (he loved playing Dad':) The automatic cutoff is broken, so be sure to turn the water off. I wouldn't want it to overflow!' Amos didn't notice the storm brewing as he went off to his bed in the loft."

"I guess it wasn't scarcely an hour later that the floodwaters begun to rise, and the rain continued all night as we slept. I was the first to awaken, and hear on the radio that homes were being evacuated by helicopter. As the water level approached are loft, I shouted at Amos and scrambled through the trap door to the log roof, hoping to flag down the rescuers. Amos followed me, half asleep. Before I could get him into the chopper, he groused, 'If you would have only listened to me, this disaster wouldn't have happened.' The winds were whipping us left and right, and I was afraid we'd been tossed into the river and swept toward the pine tree downstream.

Rescuers approach to pick up the two men as the flood waters flow swiftly toward the tower past Amos and Gerald's house.

"Don't be a fool!' I shouted eagerly. 'Just get into the helicopter before we drown!' We finally settled into the chopper and were carried to safety.

"Even though we survived that fiasco without a scratch, to this day Amos refuses to own a washing machine.

Find the 17 errors in this activity.
There are no errors in the illustration or the caption.

---

23. Recipe for Destruction

The powerful, violent wind storms known as tornadoes are found in areas where large masses of rapidly moving cold, dry air overrun warm humid air. In the United States, this condition occurs most frequently in the southwest and the south during the Spring and early Summer.

When a cold front overruns a warm front. The warm air rises and the cold air descends. Large masses of rapidly rising warm, humid air (updrafts) form cumulonimbus clouds (thunderclouds). Cumulonimbus clouds reach high into the stratosphere where the air in the warm updrafts cools and descends, the resulting downdrafts carry rain.

The strong downdrafts in the thundercloud is the first ingredient in forming a tornado. The second requirement is for the air too start rotating. This occurs when a crosswind creates a shear that cuts through the cumulus cloud. The shear blows past the warm updrafts, make the air spiral, as this warm air spins faster, the spiral tightens and draws in more warm air. Eventually, a whirlpool shape is formed with spiraling updrafts surrounding an increasingly strong downdraft. The funnel of this whirlpool shape begins stretching down out of the cloud. When the funnel cloud reaches the ground, it can contain winds moving at more than 3000 miles per hour!

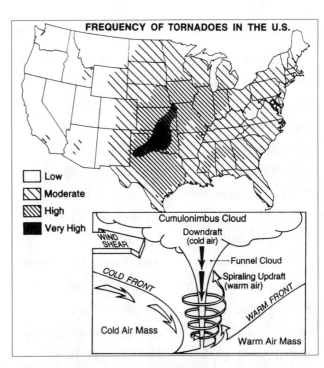

Tornadoes require two conditions to form:
1. A rapidly moving cold front overruns a warm front
   - Strong updrafts form as warm air trapped under the oncoming cold air mass tries to rise
   - Updrafts carrying warm, moist air form towering cumulonimbus clouds (thunderclouds)
2. A strong crosswind creates a shear that cuts through the cumulonimbus cloud
   - The shear causes the updrafts to spin and eventually form a whirlpool shape with spiraling updrafts surrounding a downdraft
   - The funnel of the whirlpool shape drops out of the cumulonimbus cloud
   - When the funnel cloud reaches the ground, winds in the tornado can exceed 300 m.p.h.

Find the 14 errors in this activity.
There are no errors in the illustration or the caption.

24. Placid Thrills

What a surprise I'll have for Robert on Christmas day! By then, we will flown to the Lake Placid, N.J. Olympic grounds, site of the 1922 and 1980 winter games. During the off-Olympic years, regular folks like ourselves can experience the thrill of winter events on a real Olympic course. When I bring Robert to Lake Placid, he will have a blast!

Thrill seekers may take part in any of the following (if they dare:) luge, skiing, skating, tobogganing, dogsledding, bobsledding, snowmobiling, and sleigh riding. (I almost wish there were less events to choose from! The dogsledding or snowmobiling take too long for Robert and I, but we may briefly watch a team of dogs pulling a sled and ice skaters on the rink.)

The high point of the trip will be Robert's favorite event: the fast and sometimes dangerous sport of mens' bobsledding. A four-man bobsledding team all works together in synchronization. One drives, one brakes, and the other two bob rhythmically as the sled careens down icy slopes at speeds up to 90 miles per hour.

You don't have to be a world-class athlete to enjoy the winter sports facilities at Lake Placid, N.Y. Site of two Winter Olympics (1932 and 1980), the grounds are used by sports enthusiasts from all over.

Sharp turns and a set of banked walls helps to control the sled, keeping it on course. By the time we leave Lake Placid, Robert will take the most thrilling ride of his life and will be a true "Bob"sledder! He will never forget his Olympic surprise of a lifetime.

Find the 16 errors in this activity.
There are no errors in the illustration or the caption.

---

25. Stalk Your Claim

It is 4:30 at Prouse's, and the last of the four oclock crowd had now disappeared into the storm. Gerry Sadowski's story, Count Ragula, is doing well as a thriller, and she is pleased with the signing turnout. Suddenly, the lights dim. Hands trembling Gerry signs an extra copy of her book. She is unaware of the dark shape (so like *Wicked Places'* main character)! moving stealthily towards her. A shadow crosses the page as she crosses her ts. She looks up. Her eyes pop, but her scream is cut off.

"I'm sorry to disturb you, Miss Scott," says John Aziz. With a sweep of his tattered cape (he has dressed in costume to convince the author of his enthusiasm, he opens his arms imploringly. "Would you be kind enough to advise me on publishing some work of my own"?

The store lights brighten as Gerry sighs with relief. "I-I'd be glad to," she stammers, still a little flustered. She gains momentum. "You must sink your teeth into your work. The principle key to success is dedication, so if I was you, I'd go to the writers' class I'm teaching next week. I'll be here only 15 minutes more, but if

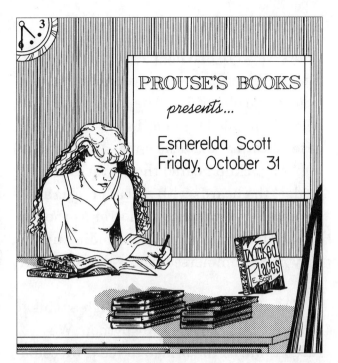

Gerry Sadowski uses her pen name, Esmerelda Scott, to sign autographs at Prouse's from 3 to 5 P.M. today. Her story, originally entitled "Count Ragula," is now sold as the book *Wicked Places*.

you show up for "Writers Which Write," I'll teach you to inject excitement into the lifeblood of your project."

"Alright!" John exclaims. Out in the storm, he congratulates himself. "Today, I have found a mentor by capitalizing on Friday the 13th; next month, I will learn the 'Write' way to publish my how-to article, 'Opportunity Stalks'."

Find the 16 errors in this activity.
There are no errors in the illustration or the caption.

---

26. Double Take

As we were driving past Anderson Slough yesterday, we saw alot of commotion on the old bridge. The bridge had been abandoned for months yet there were several cars and trucks on it.

As a pickup neared the center of the bridge, the boards with a deafening crack gave way. We watched in horror as the car fell abruptly into the slough, ending up only partial immersed because it was high tide.

The driver climbed out though a window and clung to a nearby python. We raced towards the bridge to see if we could help. As we ran onto the bridge, someone yelled "cut, cut!" Looking around, there were several pieces of equipment along the shore. We had stumbled onto the set of a movie, and had almost taken on starring roles!

The crew was busy yelling directions to each other, so we stop to quietly watch as

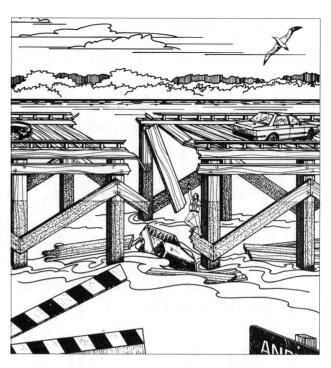

We were horrified to see a truck plunge off the old bridge into the slough; luckily, the driver was able to get out and swim to a nearby pylon.

they proceeded to film the driver's rescue. If we would have known about the film, we would have dressed for the occasion!

Find the 16 errors in this activity.
There are no errors in the illustration or the caption.

27. Granting Health

August 15, 1993

Dr. Gloria Lin Director
American Geriatric Association
113 Ringwood Drive
Houston, TX, 77111

Dear dr. Lin,

No one wants too see a child die of a heart attack. The St. George Institute is leading the fight against cholesterol disorders that can claim young lives.

Although some forms of cholesterol disorders can be treated with diet and drugs the lethal form of familial hypercholesterolemia is a more serious phenomena. Mutated genes produce an abnormal form of the low-density-lipoprotein (LDL) receptor. The liver is rendered incapable of removing LDL from the blood. As a result, patients as young as ten years old develop arteriosclerosis, which can lead to fatal heart attacks and strokes.

Thanks to your June, 92 grant of $50,000, our team were able to complete research that enabled us to provide gene therapy to three patients. The results bode well for more widespread treatment. In fact with your grant of $300,000, the St. George Institute of Molecular Research could extend its treatment capabilities to the international community.

The accompanying application details the research, procedures, and follow-up

Hoping to be awarded a $500,000 grant, Dr. Jackson sent the adjoining letter to the American Genetic Association. Above, Dr. Jackson poses after receiving the award, which she will use to expand facilities for the treatment of familial hypercholesterolemia at the St. George Institute of Molecular Research.

activities that we have implemented. Two independent analysis of our plans for facilities expansion, as well as the projected increase in treatment capability, is included. The enclosed vitae list the backgrounds and past experience of my clinical team.

Your consideration is greatly appreciated.

Sincerely;

Claudia A. Jackson

Claudia A. Jackson, Ph.D.

Find the 16 errors in this activity.
There are no errors in the illustration or the caption.

---

28. It's Never Too Late

Do you ever think, "If I was more energetic, I'd start exercising?" Although people often feel this way, it's never too late to start exercising. Seniors who start exercise programs are surprised to find that their energy level increases, and that heart and expiration rates improve. Increased weight loss is also a benefit; brisk walking for 30 minutes can burn 350 calories. In some instances, existing health problems such as adult onset diabetes has improved after the implementation of an exercise program. According to a long-term study of Harvard graduates, middle-aged and older men, who take up moderately vigorous exercise, have up to a 41% reduction in coronary artery disease. Another study indicates that this may keep arteries more flexible, lessening the degree of arterial hardening in older athletes.

Scientists have discovered that weight-bearing exercise can help to decrease the effects of osteoporosis, a loss of bone mass especially common in older women. The *Journal of the American Medical Association* reported the results of an eight-week weight-training program for a group of 86 to 96 year old's, the group improved its muscle strength,

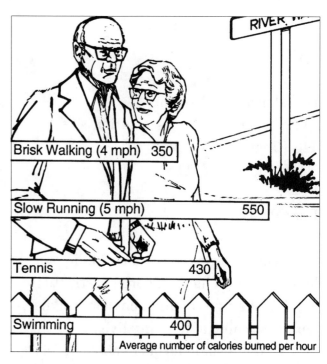

Brisk Walking (4 mph)	350
Slow Running (5 mph)	550
Tennis	430
Swimming	400

Average number of calories burned per hour

Seniors who engage in an exercise program can lose weight and improve their heart and respiration rates. Weight-training can help to prevent osteoporosis.

which enabled them to become more mobile and self-sufficient.

Scientists have conclude that many of what we consider the "normal symptoms of aging" may be in part symptoms of inactivity. The progressive dysfunction associated with aging may be postponed somewhat by regular aerobic exercise. Scientists expect that further benefits of exercise will be revealed as research continues.

Find the 15 errors in this activity.
There are no errors in the illustration or the caption.

---

29. Drawing on Psychology

The question is Which posts are farther away? In reality, we know that all of the "posts" are from our eyes the same distance. They are simply marks on a two-dimensional page. On the other hand, when drawn with the proper surroundings, the smaller posts will appear further away. Psychological affects such as perceptual context allows the artist to fool the observer into seeing two dimensions. (Here, the artist has made the first post 120% of the size of the second in order to create the illusion of distance).

Psychology works both ways. Most of us let our knowledge of real size effect our drawing, the resulting pictures appear unrealistically. The artist must constantly be vigilant in order to draw things as they appear not as they are known to really be. Farther, an artist must maintain their vigilance, as well as enthusiasm, through many trials and errors. You might say that artists really have to get "psyched!

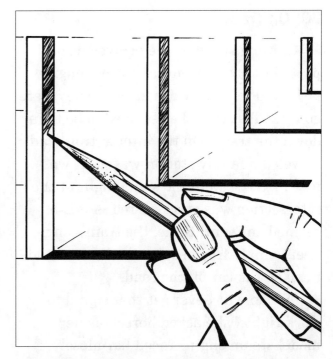

Like other pictures, the illustration above is drawn in two dimensions. An observer, however, uses the relative sizes of objects to interpret differences in distance and "see" three dimensions. The illusion of depth can also be created by artists' techniques such as shading.

Find the 16 errors in this activity.
There are no errors in the illustration or the caption.

---

30. On Track

Gaining speed as they traveled south past Hockett Station was the old engine #678 and its five attached cars. They were going so fast that they seemed to be flying down the track. On the intersecting road, traveled a family station wagon. It was now 9:15 A.M., and the signal light at the intersection was stuck on red. A crash seemed eminent! Rosie, the train's engineer, simply frowned, reached down, and plucked the car off the road.

"When will I ever get that signal to work right," she asked herself as her model steam engine raced harmlessly past. "It's anyones guess as to when I'll get the time. Right now I have other things to deal with."

She took the broken, red caboose from the track where it laid and placed it on a track, where it was out of the way. Various other tasks awaited her attention rebuilding a failing engine, creating new landscape pieces, and laying track for a new route. For Rosie and her brothers, Nick and Theodore, these kind of tasks were a labor of love.

Of the three siblings, Nick was first to

Rosie has created a realistic railroad scene, right down to the positioning of her fake morning sun. She has also linked the movements of road vehicles to the traffic signals. At 9:15 A.M., the above traffic signal is stuck on green; the train and an approaching car seem doomed to collide.

begin the model railroad hobby; after her brother, Theodore, became enthusiastic, Rosie picked it up. "It's not a childrens' game, and it is a lot of work," say the three, but we would never give up the railroading life!

Find the 15 errors in this activity.
There are no errors in the illustration or the caption.

---

31. Scheduled for Success

Moira is aware that, in today's competitive world, the straight-A student or top-ranked athlete are no longer assured of acceptance at a top university (such as an Ivy League school;) admissions officers are looking for qualified well-rounded applicants. Moira is a honor roll student taking seven college preparatory classes this semester and participating on the school debate team. She would also like to try out for the soccer team, which practices Tuesday and Thursday, but she already has a flute lesson on Tuesday. In order to add more activities to her busy schedule and leave some free time for her, Moira will have to manage her time efficiently.

First Moira lists her activities for Tuesday. Then she tries to determine how to schedule them all. Tryouts for the soccer team is at 4:00. Moira's flute lesson is at 5:30, but it is across town, and she will have to take the bus to get there. Moira is also working on a group history project, and everyone is expected to bring their part of the project to a meeting Tuesday night at 6:30. The group is meeting at a classmate's house near Moira's flute teachers so she can walk or take the bus to her meeting.

If Moira leaves the soccer tryouts at 5:00, she can like take the 5:10 bus from

4 Valley View			4
Comes From Line	Valley View High Ⓐ	19th & Oak Ⓑ	Oak & Elm Ⓒ	Elm & Maple Ⓓ

MONDAY — SATURDA

Read Across →				
5	5:10	—	5:25	—
G	5:20	5:25	5:35	5:40
5	5:30	—	5:45	—
G	5:40	5:45	5:55	6:00
5	5:50		6:05	—
G	6:00	6:05	6:15	6:20
	6:10	—	6:25	

Moira bases her schedule on the city bus times and routes to coordinate her Tuesday activities. Because her history group happens to be meeting near the home of her flute teacher, Moira can fit all her activities into her schedule.

school to the corner of Oak and Elm, arriving at 5:25, and then walk to her teacher's house on Oak Street. If she is late leaving the tryouts, she can take the next bus, which leaves school at 5:20. This will drop her at Oak and Elm at 5:25. Her classmate's house is six blocks away on Maple. If Moira finishes her flute lesson by 6:00, she can walk to the meeting, if her flute lesson runs late, she will have caught the 6:15 bus at the corner of Oak and Elm and the bus will drop her at Maple and Elm by 6:20.

Find the 15 errors in this activity.
There are no errors in the illustration or the caption.

32. An Honest Fake

Nothing but darkness meets his gaze. Only the fresh breath of spring fills Les Anyman's nostrils as he staggers stiffly to his feet and works his wrists free from their bonds. He takes off his mask. He is all by him in the woods. Next to him on the damp stones lie an envelope. He reads the following:

If you want to be one
Of the guys whom has fun
Then you must walk the earth
To show ourselves your worth
Bring back the stuff
To prove you have enough
Of what it will take
To be an Honest Fake

"This is someones idea of a test," Les thinks, racking his brain. Get into the Honest Fakes is an honor, but you have to have animal magnetism and charm. You have to be able to carry a tune. You have to have good looks. In fact, you must be a capital fellow all around. Les wonders if he can measure up? Suddenly, he knows what to do!

From the park, Les heads east to the Five and Dime and finds a small refrigerator magnet in the shape of a cow. The next stop is the bookstore, where he buys a comic book and some note paper. (He also gets a list of cities including Albany, N.Y., San Francisco, California and Jackson, Mississippi). He then drops by the

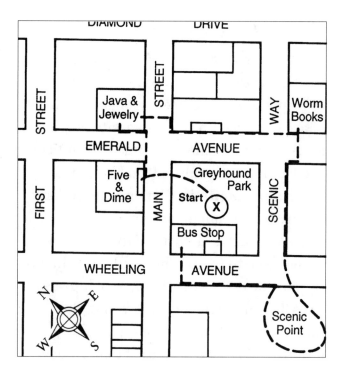

The Honest Fakes blindfold Les and take him from their clubhouse to Greyhound Park. The map above shows Les's trail starting from the park. He gathers the following tokens to represent his qualifications for the Honest Fakes club: a cow magnet (animal magnetism), a charm bracelet (charm), a comic book (carry a "toon"), a list of state capitals (capital fellow), and a drawing of beautiful scenery (good looks). When he is finished, he returns to the clubhouse and presents himself in his best formal English.

jeweler's to pick up a charm bracelet. At the scenic point, he takes several "good looks" at the surrounding area and sketches them onto the note paper. He is now ready to head Northwest to get the return bus to the clubhouse. He can hardly wait to knock on the clubhouse door. "It is me," he will say, "The newest member of the Honest Fakes."

**Find the 17 errors in this activity.
There are no errors in the illustration or the caption.**

33. Moore Money

Carlos Moore, Assistant Manager at a fast-food restaurant, makes $5.00 an hour and works 15 hours a week. He also gets $15.00 a week doing the yard work, laundry etc. at home. Currently, Carlos takes the bus to, and from work. He has decided to buy his own "wheels;" as a result he needs to budget carefully to cover the additional expenses.

Carlos is given free meals at work so he can cut down his food expenses; however he still likes to eat out two or three times a week. On weekends, he goes to the movies ($7.00) or bowls two games ($2.50 shoes, $2.50/game.) Sometimes he goes to the school basketball game ($5.00). He usually spends extra money on snacks. When he's out. Each week, he allows $10.00 for school supplies such as stationary and $10.00 for miscellaneous personal expenses. He puts $20.00 weekly in to a college savings plan. He plans to split the cost of the car with his parents; he will be responsible for half the car payment ($68.00 weekly) and half the insurance ($6.25 weekly), plus gas.

Having list all the prospective costs, planning a budget is next. The pie charts show Carlos's current weekly expenses

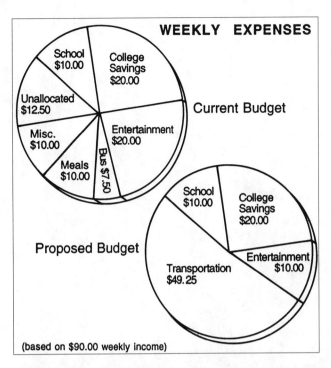

WEEKLY EXPENSES

Current Budget

Proposed Budget

(based on $90.00 weekly income)

Carlos will split the $272 monthly car payments with his parents. He will pay $6.25 weekly for his insurance and is budgeting $9.00 weekly for gas.

and his proposed expenses if he gets a car. In order to meet his additional costs, Carlos will have to eliminate about $50.00 from his current weekly expenses. He does not want to touch the money for his college savings fund. He can easily eliminate the meals out and cut his entertainment costs by a third. Carlos feels that it's worth "tightening his belt" if he can "broaden his horizons."

Find the 16 errors in this activity.
There are no errors in the illustration or the caption.

ANSWERS

This answer key provides the following information for each activity: the number and types of errors, a paragraph using superscribed numbers to show the locations of the errors, a corresponding number key explaining the errors, and the corrected paragraph.

Note that in the error count below, a run-on sentence or a sentence fragment is counted as one error even though the

correction may require two changes, e.g., adding or deleting a period and a capital letter.

The errors in English mechanics in *Editor in Chief C1* have been geared to correspond to an advanced-level English curriculum. For further information about the rules of grammar, usage, and punctuation covered in this book, see the *Guide* pp. 75–124.

1. American First Ladies

11 errors—2 content; 9 punctuation

American First Ladies Errors

Presidential first ladies have been an active force in American politics for about 300[1] years. These womens'[2] roles have been many,[3] and varied[4] In 1800, Abigail Adams, dubbed "Mrs. President",[5] was a fervent activist against antifederalists. Sarah Polk served as President James Polk's chief aide during his term in the 1830s.[6] As an outspoken abolitionist, Mary Lincoln had an enormous influence on President Lincoln's policies.

Eleanor Roosevelt[7] remembered as one of the most publicly active first ladies, worked in support of the New Deal and integration and was the first of the first ladies to testify before Congress,[8] she was particularly famous for her worldwide humanitarian work and was elected to chair the United Nation's[9] Human Rights Commission in 1946[10] helping to draft the Universal Declaration of Human Rights.

Rosalynn Carter was Jimmy's political partner during his term from 1977 to 1981. She supervised the Commission on Mental Health and helped to draft the Mental Health Systems Act of 1980.

Presidential wives have been playing

an active[11] vital role throughout American political history. In the future, perhaps all presidential spouses will continue to do so.

1. *200* years—Content: see time line (also caption: *since the earliest years of the republic*) **[2.1]**
2. *women's* role—Punctuation: *'s* used with possessive of plural not ending. in *s* **[5.6]**
3. *many* and varied—Punctuation: comma unnecessary **[5.41 b]**
4. *varied.*—Punctuation: period used after declarative sentence **[5.52]**
5. "Mrs. *President,*"—Punctuation: comma falls inside quotation marks **[5.40]**
6. in the *1840s*—Content: see illustration **[2.1]**
7. Eleanor *Roosevelt,* remembered as—Punctuation: comma used with nonessential participial phrase **[5.31]**
8. *Congress. She* was—Punctuation: period corrects comma splice **[5.52, 5.81]**
9. United *Nations'*—Punctuation: apostrophe used with possessive of plural ending in *s* **[5.5]**
10. in *1946,* helping—Punctuation: comma used with nonessential participial phrase **[5.31]**
11. *active,* vital role—Punctuation:

comma used with coordinate adjectives **[5.24]**
(Acceptable: active *and* vital)

American First Ladies Corrected

Presidential first ladies have been an active force in American politics for about 200 years. These women's roles have been many and varied. In 1800, Abigail Adams, dubbed "Mrs. President," was a fervent activist against antifederalists. Sarah Polk served as President James Polk's chief aide during his term in the 1840s. As an outspoken abolitionist, Mary Lincoln had an enormous influence on President Lincoln's policies.

Eleanor Roosevelt, remembered as one of the most publicly active first ladies, worked in support of the New Deal and integration and was the first of the first ladies to testify before Congress. She was particularly famous for her worldwide humanitarian work and was elected to chair the United Nations' Human Rights Commission in 1946, helping to draft the Universal Declaration of Human Rights.

Rosalynn Carter was Jimmy's political partner during his term from 1977 to 1981. She supervised the Commission on Mental Health and helped to draft the Mental Health Systems Act of 1980.

Presidential wives have been playing an active, vital role throughout American political history. In the future, perhaps all presidential spouses will continue to do so.

2. History of the Dome

12 errors—3 content; 1 capitalization; 2 grammar; 4 punctuation; 1 spelling; 1 usage

History of the Dome Errors

From the simplest wigwam to the more[1] magnificent cathedral, the dome is a form of architecture that has been around for centuries. The Indian stupa, originally an earthen burial mound, evolved into a domed structure in the

First Century[2] B.C. (Still standing today are[3] the tallest and finest of the stupas, the Great Stupa.) Ancient Assyrians, Parisians,[4] and Romans were the first to constructing[5] buildings with dome rooves.[6] The sides of those early buildings were rounded or polygonal.

In the A.D. 500s, the Byzantine architects developed pendentive construction, providing a dynamic solution to the problem of setting a round dome.[7] Atop a square or rectangular building. The top dome rests upon a larger dome from which the top and four corner[8] segments have been removed (see diagram.[9]) The Hagia Sophia, built in Constantinople between 532 and 537 B.C.[10], is one of the supreme achievements in world architecture[11] and it offers a prime example of pendentive construction. Light flows through forty windows,[12] that encircle the base of the dome, giving the illusion that the dome is suspended in space.

1. *most magnificent*—Grammar: superlative adjective (also parallel structure) **[3.6, 4.14]**
2. *first century*—Capital: unnecessary **[1.4, 1.5]**
3. today *is*—Usage: agreement of verb with subject (tallest and finest/is) Note: we know the subject is singular because of its singular appositive *Great Stupa* **[4.3]**
4. *Persians,*—Content: see caption (Persia) **[2.1]**
5. *to construct*—Grammar: infinitive **[3.39]**
6. *roofs*—Spelling **[6.3]**
7. *dome atop*—Punctuation: sentence fragment **[5.82]**
8. four *rim* segments—Content: see caption and illustration **[2.1]** (Acceptable: *side* segments)
9. *diagram*).—Punctuation: period outside parenthesis **[5.55]**
10. 537 *A.D.*—Content: see caption (the Byzantines built in the 500s A.D.) **[2.1]**

11. *architecture,* and—Punctuation: comma used before coordinating conjunction joining independent clauses **[5.37]**
12. *windows* that—Punctuation: comma unnecessary in essential appositive **[5.41 i]**

History of the Dome Corrected

From the simplest wigwam to the most magnificent cathedral, the dome is a form of architecture that has been around for centuries. The Indian stupa, originally an earthen burial mound, evolved into a domed structure in the first century B.C. (Still standing today is the tallest and finest of the stupas, the Great Stupa.) Ancient Assyrians, Persians, and Romans were the first to construct buildings with dome roofs. The sides of those early buildings were rounded or polygonal.

In the A.D. 500s, the Byzantine architects developed pendentive construction, providing a dynamic solution to the problem of setting a round dome atop a square or rectangular building. The top dome rests upon a larger dome from which the top and four rim segments have been removed (see diagram). The Hagia Sophia, built in Constantinople between 532 and 537 A.D., is one of the supreme achievements in world architecture, and it offers a prime example of pendentive construction. Light flows through forty windows that encircle the base of the dome, giving the illusion that the dome is suspended in space.

3. An Inspirational Pitch

13 errors—3 content; 2 grammar; 7 punctuation; 1 usage

An Inspirational Pitch Errors

There are many outstanding athletes in every sport, but few has[1] been able to overcome a handicap and succeed to the degree that Jim Abbott has; he epitomizes the word "hero".[2] Jim was born on Sept.

19, 1967[3] with only one hand, yet he has managed to win a gold medal in baseball at the 1988 Winter[4] Olympics and become a major league pitcher for the California Angels and the New York Mets[5].

Jim was fitted with a prosthetic hand at age five but found it awkward and stopped using it by age six. He has never wore[6] an artificial limb since. Instead, his father devised a technique, now known as the "Abbott switch",[7] that enabled Jim to field the ball without using any artificial device. While he throws the ball with his left hand, he balances his glove on his right wrist; on the follow-through, he slips his hand into the glove to field the ball,[8] after catching a ball, he tucks the glove under his right arm, rolls the ball down his left arm, and throws. Perfecting this technique,[9] required hours of practice for his dad and he.[10] He is now so accomplished at these maneuvers,[11] that people watching him for the first time don't realize he is one-armed[12].

For Jim, the high point in his career was the no-hitter he pitched in September,[13] 1993 against the Cleveland Indians. It embodied Jim's philosophy: "I don't go out there to be courageous or inspirational. I go out there to get hitters out."

1. few *have*—Usage: agreement of verb with indefinite pronoun **[4.8]**
2. *hero.*"—Punctuation: period falls inside quotation marks **[5.54]**
3. Sept. 19, *1967,* with—Punctuation: comma used after year (month day, year,) in sentence **[5.18]**
4. *Summer* Olympics—Content: see caption (August 1988 Olympics) **[2.1]**
5. New York *Yankees*—Content: see caption **[2.1]**
6. has never *worn*—Grammar: past participle (used in present perfect tense) **[3.27, 3.29]**
7. *switch,*"—Punctuation: comma falls inside quotation marks **[5.40]**
8. *ball;* after—Punctuation: semicolon

separates clauses (in a series) containing commas (corrects comma splice)
[5.70]
(Acceptable: *field. After*)

9. *technique* required—Punctuation:
comma unnecessary before verb
[5.41 e]

10. for his dad and *him*—Grammar:
pronoun used as object **[3.22]**

11. *maneuvers* that—Punctuation: comma
unnecessary when dependent clause
follows main clause **[5.41 l]**

12. one-*handed*—Content: see caption
[2.1]

13. *September* 1993—Punctuation: comma
unnecessary between month and year
[5.41 a]

An Inspirational Pitch Corrected

There are many outstanding athletes
in every sport, but few have been able to
overcome a handicap and succeed to the
degree that Jim Abbott has; he epitomizes
the word "hero." Jim was born on Sept. 19,
1967, with only one hand, yet he has
managed to win a gold medal in baseball
at the 1988 Summer Olympics and become
a major league pitcher for the California
Angels and the New York Yankees.

Jim was fitted with a prosthetic hand
at age five but found it awkward and
stopped using it by age six. He has never
worn an artificial limb since. Instead, his
father devised a technique, now known as
the "Abbott switch," that enabled Jim to
field the ball without using any artificial
device. While he throws the ball with his
left hand, he balances his glove on his
right wrist; on the follow-through, he slips
his hand into the glove to field the ball;
after catching a ball, he tucks the glove
under his right arm, rolls the ball down
his left arm, and throws. Perfecting this
technique required hours of practice for
his dad and him. He is now so accomplished at these maneuvers that people
watching him for the first time don't
realize he is one-handed.

For Jim, the high point in his career
was the no-hitter he pitched in September
1993 against the Cleveland Indians. It
embodied Jim's philosophy: "I don't go out
there to be courageous or inspirational. I
go out there to get hitters out."

4. Flight of Fantasy

11 errors—1 content; 3 grammar; 5 punctuation;
2 usage

Flight of Fantasy Errors

"He maneuvered his small jetstar into
a crevice below the edge of the canyon. He
hoped to avoid being seen by the patrol
ships circling overhead in the vivid
Nebulean sky,[1] he knew he will[2] be unable
to last long in a fight. Suddenly, they
spotted him. He thrust his craft into high
speed and dove into the canyon, hoping to
outmaneuver[3] if not outrun[3] his pursuers.
The small ship banked sharply from side
to side, dodging speeding missiles and
jutting rocks. Squeezing the ship through
a narrow opening among[4] two rocks, he
barely managed to escape the larger patrol ship following them[5]."

As exciting as the above scenario
seems, it is not possible outside of the
movies. Some spacecraft, such as the
space shuttle, are designed to fly like
airplanes in Earths[6] atmosphere, but they
would not be able to fly this way in the
vacuum of open space. In order to bank
(tilt laterally and inwardly in flight), a
spaceship would require air to create lift
on the wings; it could not bank in outer
space because space lacks the air pressure
needed for lift. It would also be difficult
for a[7] actual spaceship to make sudden
changes in direction; changed[8] direction, a
spaceship relies on the thrust created by
rocket engines. The pilot first has to shut
down the rocket engines,[9] that are pushing the spaceship in one direction,[10] he
then ignites a set of rockets located on the
same[11] side from the direction in which he

wants to go. This lack of maneuverability would make for very slow-paced action scenes if the movies were true-to-life.

1. *sky;* he—Punctuation: semicolon separates main clauses joined without coordinating conjunction (corrects comma splice) **[5.68]**
(Acceptable: sky *because* he OR *sky. He*)
2. he knew he *would*—Grammar: after a past tense verb, use *would*, not *will* **[3.31]**
3. *outmaneuver,* if not *outrun,*—Punctuation: commas with contrasting expressions **[5.34]**
4. *between* two rocks—Usage: word pair (among/between) **[4.18]**
5. following *him.*"—Usage: agreement of pronoun with noun (he/him) **[4.2]**
6. *Earth's*—Punctuation: *'s* used with singular possessive (Earth's atmosphere)
(Also caption and context of article) **[5.4]**
7. *an* actual—Grammar: article *a* before vowel sound **[3.5]**
8. *to change* direction—Grammar: verbal (infinitive used as adverb) **[3.39]**
9. *engines* that—Punctuation: comma unnecessary with essential phrase **[5.41 i]**
10. *direction;*—Punctuation: semicolon separates main clauses joined without coordinating conjunction (corrects comma splice) **[5.68]**
11. the *side opposite*—Content: see diagram **[2.1]**
(Acceptable: the *opposite* side)

Flight of Fantasy Corrected

"He maneuvered his small jetstar into a crevice below the edge of the canyon. He hoped to avoid being seen by the patrol ships circling overhead in the vivid Nebulean sky; he knew he would be unable to last long in a fight. Suddenly, they spotted him. He thrust his craft into high speed and dove into the canyon, hoping to outmaneuver, if not outrun, his pursuers. The small ship banked sharply from side to side, dodging speeding missiles and jutting rocks. Squeezing the ship through a narrow opening between two rocks, he barely managed to escape the larger patrol ship following him."

As exciting as the above scenario seems, it is not possible outside of the movies. Some spacecraft, such as the space shuttle, are designed to fly like airplanes in Earth's atmosphere, but they would not be able to fly this way in the vacuum of open space. In order to bank (tilt laterally and inwardly in flight), a spaceship would require air to create lift on the wings; it could not bank in outer space because space lacks the air pressure needed for lift. It would also be difficult for an actual spaceship to make sudden changes in direction; to change direction, a spaceship relies on the thrust created by rocket engines. The pilot first has to shut down the rocket engines that are pushing the spaceship in one direction; he then ignites a set of rockets located on the side opposite from the direction in which he wants to go. This lack of maneuverability would make for very slow-paced action scenes if the movies were true-to-life.

5. Pirate Spiders

13 errors—3 content; 1 capitalization; 3 grammar; 2 punctuation; 1 spelling; 3 usage

Pirate Spiders Errors

The group of arachnids known as cannibal spiders, or pirate spiders[1] feed on other spiders. They belong to the family Mitosis[2]. About a dozen mimetid species live in the United States. The Black Widow[3] spider is not[4] included among them.

Many of these spiders is[5] small, about a quarter of an inch or more[6] in length.

Their bodies are delicately marked with dark lines and spots. The front pairs of legs have a series of long and short spines that the spider uses to grasp its victim firmly.

The pirate spider moves slow[7] and stealthily to captured[8] it's[9] prey. It enters the web of another spider and pulls on a line of the web. The unknowing spider, who[10] will have hurry[11] anxiously[12] to the spot in anticipation of a good meal, is caught by surprise. The pirate attacks it, injecting a poisonous venom that paralyzes its victim[13] and then slowly sucks the juices from the body of the unlucky spider.

1. *spiders,*—Punctuation: comma used with nonessential appositive (see caption) **[5.29]**
2. *Mimetidae*—Content: see caption **[2.1]**
3. *black widow* spider—Capital: unnecessary (not used as proper adjective; also, see caption) **[1.5]**
4. *is* included—Content: see caption **[2.1]**
5. *are*—Usage: agreement of verb with indefinite pronoun (many/are) **[4.8]**
6. *less*—Content: see caption **[2.1]**
7. moves *slowly*—Grammar: adverb modifies verb **[3.4]**
8. to *capture*—Grammar: verbal (infinitive used as adverb) **[3.39]**
9. *its*—Spelling (possessive) **[6.1]**
10. *which*—Usage: agreement of pronoun with antecedent **[4.2]**
11. will have *hurried*—Grammar: past participle (used in future perfect tense) **[3.27, 3.29]** (Acceptable: which *hurries*)
12. hurried *eagerly*—Usage: word pair (anxious/eager) **[4.18]**
13. *victim,* and—Punctuation: comma used with nonessential phrase **[5.31]**

Pirate Spiders Corrected

The group of arachnids known as cannibal spiders, or pirate spiders, feed on other spiders. They belong to the family Mimetidae. About a dozen mimetid species live in the United States. The black widow spider is included among them.

Many of these spiders are small, about a quarter of an inch or less in length. Their bodies are delicately marked with dark lines and spots. The front pairs of legs have a series of long and short spines that the spider uses to grasp its victim firmly.

The pirate spider moves slowly and stealthily to capture its prey. It enters the web of another spider and pulls on a line of the web. The unknowing spider, which will have hurried eagerly to the spot in anticipation of a good meal, is caught by surprise. The pirate attacks it, injecting a poisonous venom that paralyzes its victim, and then slowly sucks the juices from the body of the unlucky spider.

6. On His Toes

14 errors—2 content; 2 capitalization; 4 grammar; 4 punctuation; 1 spelling; 1 usage

On His Toes Errors

Detective Novak had finally solved a rash of apartment house burglaries that had been plaguing the area for months. "How were you able to crack this case[1] Detective?" asked the reporter.

"We have had a possible suspect for months, but he had always managed to elude us, leaving no obvious evidence behind. [2]Him and me[2] were waging a personal battle, but he was not as smart as me[3]. I knew he will[4] get careless. I was finally able to retrace his steps",[5] said the Detective[6].[7] "From[8] his shoes. Both had clues on its[9] toes."

The detective then proceeded to explain his strategy to the reporter.

"As I was questioning the suspect, I noticed a small drop of pizza sauce on the tip of his left[10] shoe. A pizza delivery boy had recall[11] that as he was arriving to deliver a pizza on the evening of the burglary, he collided with a man rushing out of the apartment building."

"But how did you place the suspect inside the burglarized apartment"?[12]

"Our suspect uses a unique brand of foot powder that is sold only in one local shop. The soul[13] of his right[14] shoe is separated at the toe, and some of his foot powder dribbled onto the carpeting. I was able to remove a small amount of powder and match it to the residue in his shoe."

"I guess a good detective always has to think on his feet," the reporter observed wryly.

1. this *case,* Detective?"—Punctuation: comma used with noun of address **[5.27]**
2. *He and I* were—Grammar: pronouns used as subjects **[3.22]**
3. as smart as *I*—Grammar: pronoun following *as* in incomplete construction (verb implied—as smart as I am) **[3.24]**
4. knew he *would* get—Grammar: past tense **[3.29]**
5. his *steps,"*—Punctuation: comma falls inside quotation marks **[5.40]**
6. the *detective*—Capital: unnecessary **[1.8]**
7. *detective,* "from—Punctuation: comma separates quote from speaker **[5.39]**
8. *"from* his shoes..."—Capital: unnecessary (divided quotation) **[1.2]**
9. on *their* toes—Usage: agreement of possessive pronoun with indefinite pronoun (both/their) **[4.9]**
10. his *right* shoe—Content: see caption and illustration **[2.1]**
11. had *recalled*—Grammar: past participle (used in past perfect tense) **[3.27, 3.29]**
12. *apartment?"*—Punctuation: quoted question **[5.58]**
13. *sole*—Spelling **[6.1]**
14. his *left* shoe—Content: see illustration **[2.1]**

On His Toes Corrected

Detective Novak had finally solved a rash of apartment house burglaries that had been plaguing the area for months.

"How were you able to crack this case, Detective?" asked the reporter.

"We have had a possible suspect for months, but he had always managed to elude us, leaving no obvious evidence behind. He and I were waging a personal battle, but he was not as smart as I. I knew he would get careless. I was finally able to retrace his steps," said the detective, "from his shoes. Both had clues on their toes."

The detective then proceeded to explain his strategy to the reporter.

"As I was questioning the suspect, I noticed a small drop of pizza sauce on the tip of his right shoe. A pizza delivery boy had recalled that as he was arriving to deliver a pizza on the evening of the burglary, he collided with a man rushing out of the apartment building."

"But how did you place the suspect inside the burglarized apartment?"

"Our suspect uses a unique brand of foot powder that is sold only in one local shop. The sole of his left shoe is separated at the toe, and some of his foot powder dribbled onto the carpeting. I was able to remove a small amount of powder and match it to the residue in his shoe."

"I guess a good detective always has to think on his feet," the reporter observed wryly.

7. Lightning Strikes Out

15 errors—2 content; 1 capitalization; 1 grammar; 8 punctuation; 1 spelling; 2 usage

Lightning Strikes Out Errors

"We have beautiful Fall[1] weather for today's state fair charity race featuring an outstanding array of horses. The horses are starting to get in position,[2] some is[3] already lined up at the gate.

"There[4] off! Greenoak Fields[5] White Lightning is in the lead with George Kantor's Fancy Free close on his heels. As they round the corner[6] Fancy Free tries to take the lead. It's Fancy Free and White Lightning. Coming up on the outside is Fleet Feet from Oakdale Stables, battling with Quickstep.

"This is a close race[7] folks. Fleet Feet surges ahead of Quickstep and is trying to overtake the leaders. The question is[8] Would[9] she be able to catch up.[10] Fancy Free and White Lightning are neck and tail[11]. Look out! White Lightning has stumbled; the crowd are[12] stunned. His riders[13] still on, but the delay has cost him the race. Fleet Feet and Fancy Free are crossing the line, [14]second and first.[14] What a loss for White Lightning.[15]

1. *fall* weather—Capital: unnecessary **[1.12]**
2. *position;* some—Punctuation: semicolon separates main clauses joined without coordinating conjunction (corrects comma splice) **[5.68]**
3. some *are*—Usage: agreement of verb with indefinite pronoun **[4.8]**
4. *They're*—Spelling (contraction) **[6.1]**
5. *Fields'*—Punctuation: apostrophe used with possessive of plural ending in *s* (see caption: Greenoak Fields) **[5.5]**
6. *corner,*—Punctuation: comma used after introductory dependent clause **[5.26]**
7. *race,* folks—Punctuation: comma used with noun of address **[5.27]**
8. question *is,*—Punctuation: comma introduces direct question within sentence **[5.35]**
9. *Will* she—Grammar: future tense **[3.29]**
10. *up?*—Punctuation: question mark used after direct question **[5.56]**
11. neck and *neck*—Content: see caption and illustration **[2.1]**
12. crowd *is*—Usage: agreement of verb with collective subject used in singular sense **[4.4]**

13. *rider's*—Punctuation: apostrophe used with contraction **[5.1]** (Acceptable: *rider is*)
14. *first and second*—Content: see caption **[2.1]**
15. *Lightning."*—Punctuation: quotation marks enclose a direct quote (final paragraph of quote spanning several paragraphs) **[5.62]** (Acceptable: *Lightning!"*)

Lightning Strikes Out Corrected

"We have beautiful fall weather for today's state fair charity race featuring an outstanding array of horses. The horses are starting to get in position; some are already lined up at the gate.

"They're off! Greenoak Fields' White Lightning is in the lead with George Kantor's Fancy Free close on his heels. As they round the corner, Fancy Free tries to take the lead. It's Fancy Free and White Lightning. Coming up on the outside is Fleet Feet from Oakdale Stables, battling with Quickstep.

"This is a close race, folks. Fleet Feet surges ahead of Quickstep and is trying to overtake the leaders. The question is, Will she be able to catch up? Fancy Free and White Lightning are neck and neck. Look out! White Lightning has stumbled; the crowd is stunned. His rider's still on, but the delay has cost him the race. Fleet Feet and Fancy Free are crossing the line, first and second. What a loss for White Lightning."

8. Setting Sail

13 errors—2 content; 1 capitalization; 2 grammar; 7 punctuation; 1 usage

Setting Sail Errors

Classes: Fridays from 4:00 P.M. to 6:00 P.M., weather permitting
Prerequisite: [1]Either completion of[1] beginning sailing or an equivalent course
Location: Shoreline Park on Surf Blvd.[2] Seattle

Wear appropriate clothing,[3] and rubber [4]soled shoes or boating shoes. Life jackets will been[5] provided. Registration is on September 10.[6]

Complete the form below, listing all previous experience in sailing or boating. Proof of completion of the Beginning Sailing[7] class (or an equivalent course,[8] will be required at the first class.

Name: _James Turner_   SSN: _000-00-000_

Address: _645 Via Nueva Avenue, Apt. 3_
Bellevue, Wash[9] 98006

Phone: _(206) 555-0029_

Age: _17_

Years of sailing experience: _6 mos[10]_

Type of experience: _I sailed a 14-foot catamaran in Hawaii and completed the beginning sailing class next[11] summer._

List the name and phone number of the person we should contact in an emergency.

Name: _Mrs. Martha Turner_

Phone: _(206) 555-8893_

Parental permission is required for students under 18.

James Turner has my permission to enroll in the advanced sailing class,[12] therefore, he can[13] participate in all course activities.

Martha Turner
Parent/Guardian

1. *Completion* of *either*—Grammar: correlative conjunctions (either/or) each followed by parallel phrase [3.15]
2. *Blvd.,* Seattle—Punctuation: comma separates elements of address [5.15]
3. *clothing* and—Punctuation: comma unnecessary in compound object [5.41 m]
4. *rubber-soled*—Punctuation: hyphen used in compound adjective [5.48]
5. will *be*—Grammar: infinitive (used in future tense) [3.27, 3.29]
6. September *21*—Content: see illustration and caption [2.1]

7. *beginning sailing*—Capital: unnecessary (school subject) [1.13]
8. *course)*—Punctuation: parentheses used (in pairs) to enclose supplementary words [5.49] (Acceptable: no parentheses)
9. *Wash.*—Punctuation: period used after abbreviation [5.53] (Acceptable: WA)
10. *mos.*—Punctuation: period used after abbreviation [5.53]
11. *last*—Content: see illustration (completion of beginning sailing is a prerequisite for registration) [2.1] (Acceptable: *this* summer)
12. *class;* therefore,—Punctuation: semicolon used before conjunctive adverb joining independent clauses [5.69]
13. *may*—Usage: word pair (can/may) [4.18]

Setting Sail Corrected

Classes: Fridays from 4:00 P.M. to 6:00 P.M., weather permitting
Prerequisite: Completion of either beginning sailing or an equivalent course
Location: Shoreline Park on Surf Blvd., Seattle

Wear appropriate clothing and rubber-soled shoes or boating shoes. Life jackets will be provided. Registration is on September 21.

Complete the form below, listing all previous experience in sailing or boating. Proof of completion of the beginning sailing class (or an equivalent course) will be required at the first class.

Name: _James Turner_   SSN: _000-00-000_

Address: _645 Via Nueva Avenue, Apt. 3_
Bellevue, Wash, 98006

Phone: _(206) 555-0029_

Age: _17_

Years of sailing experience: _6 mos._

Type of experience: _I sailed a 14-foot catamaran in Hawaii and completed the beginning sailing class last summer._

List the name and phone number of the person we should contact in an emergency.

Name: _Mrs. Martha Turner_

Phone: _(206) 555-8893_

Parental permission is required for students under 18.

James Turner has my permission to enroll in the advanced sailing class; therefore, he may participate in all course activities.

Martha Turner
Parent/Guardian

9. The Money Tree

13 errors—4 content; 1 capitalization;
2 grammar; 1 punctuation; 2 spelling; 3 usage

The Money Tree Errors

Some high school students involved in the city's 7th[1] annual park restoration and cleanup day this weekend did cleanup[2] in a real[3] big way! The students uncovered a paper bag[4] [5]while planting a tree filled with money[5]. The police, who took charge when the bag was found, believes[6] the money was stolen in a bank robbery twelve[7] years ago. The culprits were caught, but[8] never was the money found.[8]

The students who recovered the treasure, nearly $5,000[9], are hoping the bank will offer them a reward for there[10] honesty. "I've never seen so much money in my life," said one of the young men,[11] but I certainly wouldn't have any problem thinking of ways to spending[12] it. Who says money doesn't grow on trees?[11] he added. Bank Officers[13] were not available for comment.

1. _10th_ annual—Content: see illustration **[2.1]**
2. _clean up_—Spelling **[6.6]**
3. _really_ big—Grammar: adverb modifies adjective **[3.4]**
4. uncovered a _plastic_ bag—Content: see caption **[2.1]**
5. bag _filled with money_ while—Usage:

misplaced modifier **[4.15]** (Acceptable: _While planting a tree,_ the students...bag filled with money.)
6. _believe_ the money—Usage: agreement of verb with collective subject used in plural sense (police/believe) **[4.4]**
7. _twenty_—Content: see caption **[2.1]**
8. but _the money was never found._—Usage: parallel structure **[4.11]**
9. _$50,000_—Content: see caption **[2.1]**
10. _their_—Spelling **[6.1]**
11. _"but I certainly...grow on trees?"_—Punctuation: quotation marks enclose both parts of divided quotation **[5.60]**
12. _to spend_—Grammar: infinitive **[3.27]** (Acceptable: ways _of_ spending)
13. Bank _officers_—Capital: unnecessary (title without name) **[1.8]**

The Money Tree Corrected

Some high school students involved in the city's 10th annual park restoration and cleanup day this weekend did clean up in a really big way! The students uncovered a plastic bag filled with money while planting a tree. The police, who took charge when the bag was found, believe the money was stolen in a bank robbery twenty years ago. The culprits were caught, but the money was never found.

The students who recovered the treasure, nearly $50,000, are hoping the bank will offer them a reward for their honesty. "I've never seen so much money in my life," said one of the young men, "but I certainly wouldn't have any problem thinking of ways to spend it. Who says money doesn't grow on trees?" he added. Bank officers were not available for comment.

10. On Shaky Ground

16 errors—2 content; 1 capitalization;
2 grammar; 7 punctuation; 2 spelling; 2 usage

On Shaky Ground Errors

157 Faultline Drive
Golden Fields[1, 2] CA 95091
October 24, 1989

Dear Gina[3]

I know that you have been worried about us since the earthquake. Were[4] all fine, although still a little shaken up.

There was alot[5] of damage downtown. Buildings collapsed, and many fires breaked[6] out because of the broken gas lines. Tragically, several people were killed by falling rocks[7].

When the earthquake hit, I was in San Jose and couldn't get home for hours. Many freeways were closed because of structural damage, collapsing overpasses, or [8]rocks that had slid[8]; as a result, I had to drive home along back roads. The next morning I heard that after I have[9] driven home, the bridge I had crossed was declared unsafe!

My parents[10] house was a disaster area! Closets spilled their contents[11] shelves jettisoned dishes, hutches fell on their faces, and glass shards hurtled everywhere!

My Dad[12] said that everything were[13] moving so much that he couldn't even get out of his chair. I asked my mom if it was noisy with everything crashing to the floor and glass breaking. She said, "I was so scared that I didn't hear a thing".[14]

Well, I have to go now. There's still alot[15] of cleaning up to do!

Love[16]

Jose

1. *Green Meadows*—Content: see illustration and caption [2.1]
2. Green *Meadows,* CA—Punctuation: comma separates elements of address [5.15]
3. Dear *Gina,*—Punctuation: comma used after greeting of friendly letter [5.19]
4. *We're*—Punctuation: apostrophe used in contraction [5.1]
5. *a lot*—Spelling [6.6]
6. fires *broke* out—Grammar: past tense (irregular) [3.27, 3.29]

7. *bricks*—Content: see caption [2.1]
8. or *rockslides*;—Usage: parallel structure [4.11]
   (Acceptable: *sliding rocks*)
9. I *had* driven—Grammar: past participle (used in past perfect tense) [3.27, 3.29]
10. *parents'* house—Punctuation: apostrophe used with possessive of plural ending in *s* [5.5]
11. *contents,* shelves—Punctuation: commas used after independent clauses (short and parallel) [5.23]
12. my *dad*—Capital: unnecessary [1.8]
13. everything *was*—Usage: agreement of verb with indefinite pronoun [4.8]
14. hear a *thing.*"—Punctuation: period inside quotation marks [5.54]
15. *a lot*—Spelling [6.6]
16. *Love,*—Punctuation: comma used after closing of a letter [5.21]

On Shaky Ground Corrected

157 Faultline Drive
Green Meadows, CA 95091
October 24, 1989

Dear Gina,

I know that you have been worried about us since the earthquake. We're all fine, although still a little shaken up.

There was a lot of damage downtown. Buildings collapsed, and many fires broke out because of the broken gas lines. Tragically, several people were killed by falling bricks.

When the earthquake hit, I was in San Jose and couldn't get home for hours. Many freeways were closed because of structural damage, collapsing overpasses, or rockslides; as a result, I had to drive home along back roads. The next morning I heard that after I had driven home, the bridge I had crossed was declared unsafe!

My parents' house was a disaster area! Closets spilled their contents, shelves jettisoned dishes, hutches fell on their faces, and glass shards hurtled everywhere!

My dad said that everything was moving so much that he couldn't even get out of his chair. I asked my mom if it was noisy with everything crashing to the floor and glass breaking. She said, "I was so scared that I didn't hear a thing."

Well, I have to go now. There's still a lot of cleaning up to do!

Love,

Jose

11. A Nobel Endeavor

12 errors—1 content; 5 grammar; 4 punctuation; 2 usage

A Nobel Endeavor Errors

It seems ironic that the inventor of one of the world's most destructive forces would ultimately be remembered.[1] As the creator of one of the world's most endurable[2] humanitarian legacies.

In the mid-18th[3] century, nitroglycerin was the most common[4] used explosive,[5] however, nitroglycerin is highly volatile and can explode if jarred even slightly. A nitroglycerin explosion is triggered by a chemical chain reaction,[6] that is impossible to stop once it has started.

In the 1860s, Swedish chemist Alfred Nobel owned a nitroglycerin factory. It was him[7] who invented dynamite, an explosive that was safer because it could be handled more easy[8] than nitroglycerin. To create dynamite, he mixed nitroglycerin with diatomite, a porous, earthlike substance. The resulting dry mixture of nitroglycerin and diatomite were[9] more resistant to both shock and heat than was nitroglycerin alone.

Another of Nobel's inventions, the blasting cap, allowed for safer usage of it[10]. An electric current detonated the blasting cap, which then detonated the dynamite. This latter invention made a fortune for Nobel; with this fortune, he established the Nobel prizes. These an-nual awards are given to persons worldwide whom[11] have made significant contributions to the "good of humanity" in the following fields[12] chemistry, physics, physiology/medicine, literature, international peace, and economic science.

1. *remembered as*—Punctuation: sentence fragment [**5.82**]
2. most *enduring*—Usage: word pair (enduring/endurable) [**4.18**]
3. mid-*19th* century—Content: see caption (the 19th century comprises the years of the 1800s) [**2.1**]
4. most *commonly*—Grammar: superlative adverb [**3.4, 3.6**]
5. *explosive;* however,—Punctuation: semicolon used before conjunctive adverb joining independent clauses [**5.69**]
   (Acceptable: *explosive. However,*)
6. *reaction* that—Punctuation: comma unnecessary with essential clause [**5.41 i**]
7. It was *he*—Grammar: nominative case used with the verb *to be* [**3.23**]
8. *more easily*—Grammar: comparative adverb [**3.4, 3.6**]
9. *was* more—Usage: agreement of verb with subject (mixture/was) [**4.3**]
10. *dynamite*—Grammar: ambiguous pronoun reference (see caption) [**3.19**]
11. worldwide *who* have—Grammar: pronoun *who* used as subject of adjective clause [**3.26**]
12. *fields:*—Punctuation: colon introduces words that explain or illustrate [**5.12**]

A Nobel Endeavor Corrected

It seems ironic that the inventor of one of the world's most destructive forces would ultimately be remembered as the creator of one of the world's most enduring humanitarian legacies.

In the mid-19th century, nitroglycerin was the most commonly used explosive; however, nitroglycerin is highly volatile and can explode if jarred even slightly. A nitroglycerin explosion is triggered by a chemical chain reaction that is impossible to stop once it has started.

In the 1860s, Swedish chemist Alfred Nobel owned a nitroglycerin factory. It was he who invented dynamite, an explosive that was safer because it could be handled more easily than nitroglycerin. To create dynamite, he mixed nitroglycerin with diatomite, a porous, earthlike substance. The resulting dry mixture of nitroglycerin and diatomite was more resistant to both shock and heat than was nitroglycerin alone.

Another of Nobel's inventions, the blasting cap, allowed for safer usage of dynamite. An electric current detonated the blasting cap, which then detonated the dynamite. This latter invention made a fortune for Nobel; with this fortune, he established the Nobel prizes. These annual awards are given to persons worldwide who have made significant contributions to the "good of humanity" in the following fields: chemistry, physics, physiology/medicine, literature, international peace, and economic science.

12. Diamond in the "Ruff"

15 errors—3 content; 2 capitalization;
1 grammar; 6 punctuation; 1 spelling; 2 usage

Diamond in the "Ruff" Errors

Diamond[1] winner of Best in Show at the recent Newchester Kennel Club dog show[1] is top dog. The five-year-old English Setter[2] is owned and shown by Kathy Pruitt, Veterinarian[3], of Scarsdale. "This dog's a real jewel," said his[4] ecstatic owner,[5] "Diamond is this girl's best friend!".[6]

You might wonder how a dog is judged to be the best in the show?[7] First, each breed of dog is evaluated seperately[8] by an uninterested[9] judge. Judge[10] is based on breed standards for:[11] a dog's appearance, head and body structure, color and coat,

temperament, and gait; the standards are approved by the American Kennel Club. The best of each breed then goes on to the group competition. Each breed belongs to a specific group. There are seven groups: sporting, hound, working, herding, terrier, [12]and toy. The first-place dog from each breed[13] competes for Best in Show.

Even at the final level of judging, the dogs are not compared to each other but are judged according to the standards of its[14] particular breed. Therefore[15] Best in Show is awarded to the dog that is considered the best representative of its breed. Often, subtle differences in overall showmanship become critical factors in selecting the best dog.

1. *Diamond,* winner...dog *show,* is—Punctuation: commas used with non-essential appositive **[5.29]**
2. English *setter*—Capital: unnecessary **[1.4]**
3. *veterinarian*—Capital: unnecessary (title not used as part of name) **[1.8]**
4. *her* ecstatic owner—Content: see caption (if Diamond is a "mom" she must be female) **[2.1]**
5. *owner.* "Diamond—Punctuation: period used after declarative sentence **[5.52, 5.81]**
6. *friend!"*—Punctuation: avoid multiple punctuation **[5.73]**
7. *show.*—Punctuation: question mark unnecessary after indirect question **[5.57]**
8. *separately*—Spelling **[6.7]**
9. *a disinterested* judge—Usage: word pair (uninterested/disinterested) Note: *an* changes to *a* **[4.18]**
10. *Judging*—Grammar: verbal (gerund) **[3.38]**
11. *for* a—Punctuation: colon unnecessary **[5.13]**
12. terrier, *nonsporting*, and—Content: see illustration **[2.1]**
13. from each *group*—Content: see caption **[2.1]**

14. *their* particular—Usage: agreement of possessive pronoun with noun in number **[4.1]**
15. *Therefore,* Best—Punctuation: comma used after introductory word **[5.25]**

Diamond in the "Ruff" Corrected

Diamond, winner of Best in Show at the recent Newchester Kennel Club dog show, is top dog. The five-year-old English setter is owned and shown by Kathy Pruitt, veterinarian, of Scarsdale. "This dog's a real jewel," said her ecstatic owner. "Diamond is this girl's best friend!"

You might wonder how a dog is judged to be the best in the show. First, each breed of dog is evaluated separately by a disinterested judge. Judging is based on breed standards for a dog's appearance, head and body structure, color and coat, temperament, and gait; the standards are approved by the American Kennel Club. The best of each breed then goes on to the group competition. Each breed belongs to a specific group. There are seven groups: sporting, hound, working, herding, terrier, nonsporting, and toy. The first-place dog from each group competes for Best in Show.

Even at the final level of judging, the dogs are not compared to each other but are judged according to the standards of their particular breed. Therefore, Best in Show is awarded to the dog that is considered the best representative of its breed. Often, subtle differences in overall showmanship become critical factors in selecting the best dog.

13. A Horse of a Different Color

13 errors—1 content; 3 grammar; 3 punctuation; 2 spelling; 4 usage

A Horse of a Different Color Errors

The sea horse is unique in many ways. It coils its tail around plants and clings there while sucking up passing crustaceans through its pipettelike snout. It can swim weakly with its dorsal fin but usually floats along upright in the currents. The largest sea horse, *Hippocampus ingens*, can grow to 14 inches.

Certain species have also adapted their skin texture to match their environment,[1] for example, *H. bargibanti,* the smallest sea horse, has bumps that mimic the texture of corral[2]. As[3] chameleons, many species of sea horses can change color to blend in with their background. The sea horse and the chameleon also shares[4] the trait of dependent[5] eye movement; this trait helps the sea horse ambushes[6] its prey in the reefs and sea grass meadows.

Among fishes[7] the male is often the nurture[8] parent, carin g for the eggs until they hatch. Male sea horses carry this behavior one step farther[9]. The female sea horse deposits her eggs in the male's brood pouch. He then carrys[10] the eggs until they hatch as completely independent,[11] miniature sea horses.

A growing trade in sea horses, particularly in Asia, has now endanger[12] these special creatures. [13]Used primarily in pharmaceuticals,[13] the largest market for sea horses is mainland China. Dredging and pollution have also damaged many of the sea horses' coastal habitats.

1. *environment;* for example,—Punctuation: semicolon used before conjunctive adverb joining independent clauses **[5.69]**
   (Acceptable: *environment*: H. bargibanti,)
2. *coral*—Spelling **[6.7]**
3. *Like* chameleons—Usage: word pair (like/as) **[4.18]**
   (Also, caption indicates that the sea horse is not a chameleon)
4. sea horse and the chameleon also *share*—Usage: agreement of verb with two subjects joined by *and* **[4.6]**
5. *independent*—Content: see caption **[2.1]**
6. *ambush*—Grammar: infinitive **[3.27]**
   (Acceptable: *to ambush*)

7. *fishes,*—Punctuation: comma used after introductory phrase **[5.26]**

8. *nurturing*—Grammar: verbal (participle used as adjective) **[3.37]**

9. *further*—Usage: word pair (further/farther) **[4.18]**

10. *carries*—Spelling **[6.4]**

11. *independent* miniature—Punctuation: comma unnecessary between noncoordinate adjectives **[5.41 c]**

12. *endangered*—Grammar: past participle (used in present perfect tense) **[3.27, 3.29]**
(Acceptable: Asia, now *endangers*)

13. The largest...sea horses, *used primarily in pharmaceuticals,* is—Usage: misplaced modifier **[4.15]**

A Horse of a Different Color Corrected

The sea horse is unique in many ways. It coils its tail around plants and clings there while sucking up passing crustaceans through its pipettelike snout. It can swim weakly with its dorsal fin but usually floats along upright in the currents. The largest sea horse, *Hippocampus ingens*, can grow to 14 inches.

Certain species have also adapted their skin texture to match their environment; for example, *H. bargibanti,* the smallest sea horse, has bumps that mimic the texture of coral. Like chameleons, many species of sea horses can change color to blend in with their background. The sea horse and the chameleon also share the trait of independent eye movement; this trait helps the sea horse ambush its prey in the reefs and sea grass meadows.

Among fishes, the male is often the nurturing parent, caring for the eggs until they hatch. Male sea horses carry this behavior one step further. The female sea horse deposits her eggs in the male's brood pouch. He then carries the eggs until they hatch as completely independent miniature sea horses.

A growing trade in sea horses, particularly in Asia, has now endangered these special creatures. The largest market for sea horses, used primarily in pharmaceuticals, is mainland China. Dredging and pollution have also damaged many of the sea horses' coastal habitats.

14. Animal Partnerships

14 errors—1 content; 2 grammar; 7 punctuation; 4 usage

Animal Partnerships Errors

Many animals have formed a symbiotic relationship, or mutually beneficial partnership, with another species. The hermit crab's shell is not strong enough to stop a hungry octopus[1] so the crab carries sea anemones on its back for protection. The octopus or other predators avoids[2] the anemone's stinging tentacles. Protected from predators, the [3]anemone is carried[3] to new feeding areas.

The goby fish and the snapping shrimp live together as roommates and relies[4] on one another for survival. There are no[5] more than 30 kinds of gobies in partnerships with shrimp. The shrimp digs a nesting hole that provides both it and the goby with a ready[6] made escape from enemies. In exchange, the shrimp relies on the goby, which sees better, to serve as lookout. The shrimp will rest one of its antennae on the goby; if a predator approaches, the goby would[7] rapidly flick its tail[8] signaling the shrimp to hide.

In the marine world, various kinds of fish and shrimp specialize in cleaning other sea creatures,[9] a cleaner shrimp[10] for instance[10] will clean inside the mouth of a fish by removing bacteria, fungi, or tiny animals,[11] caught in the fish's teeth. The remora hitchhikes rides on:[12] sharks, rays, whales, and other sea creatures. Using a sucker on top of its head, a remora attaches itself to a host. The remora benefits from the easy access to food, using its protruding jaw to collect both scraps dropped by its host and parasites it scrapes from the host's body.

Offering a similar service on land is[13] several types of birds. The rhinoceros bird, for example, will perch on the back of the rhinoceros to eat the swarms of annoying insects that continually torment it.[14]

1. *octopus,* so—Punctuation: comma used before coordinating conjunction joining independent clauses **[5.37]**

2. predators *avoid*—Usage: agreement of verb with closer of two subjects joined by *or* **[4.6]**

3. predators, the *crab carries the anemone* to new—Usage: dangling modifier **[4.16]**

4. and *rely* on—Usage: agreement of verb with two subjects joined by *and* **[4.6]**

5. *are more* than 30—Content: see caption **[2.1]**

6. *ready-made*—Punctuation: hyphen used in compound adjective **[5.48]**

7. goby *will* rapidly flick—Grammar: helping verb (used in future tense) **[3.33]**
   (Acceptable: goby *rapidly flicks*)

8. *tail,* signaling—Punctuation: comma used with nonessential phrase **[5.31]**

9. sea *creatures;* a cleaner—Punctuation: semicolon separates main clauses joined without coordinating conjunction (corrects comma splice) **[5.68]**

10. *shrimp,* for *instance,*—Punctuation: commas used with sentence interrupter **[5.28]**

11. *animals* caught—Punctuation: unnecessary comma **[5.41 i]**

12. *on* sharks—Punctuation: colon unnecessary **[5.13]**
    (Acceptable: rides on *the following*:)

13. *are*—Usage: agreement of verb with subject (types/are) **[4.3]**

14. the *rhinoceros*—Grammar: ambiguous pronoun reference (see caption) **[3.19]**

Animal Partnerships Corrected

Many animals have formed a symbiotic relationship, or mutually beneficial partnership, with another species. The hermit crab's shell is not strong enough to stop a hungry octopus, so the crab carries sea anemones on its back for protection. The octopus or other predators avoid the anemone's stinging tentacles. Protected from predators, the crab carries the anemone to new feeding areas.

The goby fish and the snapping shrimp live together as roommates and rely on one another for survival. There are more than 30 kinds of gobies in partnerships with shrimp. The shrimp digs a nesting hole that provides both it and the goby with a ready-made escape from enemies. In exchange, the shrimp relies on the goby, which sees better, to serve as lookout. The shrimp will rest one of its antennae on the goby; if a predator approaches, the goby will rapidly flick its tail, signaling the shrimp to hide.

In the marine world, various kinds of fish and shrimp specialize in cleaning other sea creatures; a cleaner shrimp, for instance, will clean inside the mouth of a fish by removing bacteria, fungi, or tiny animals caught in the fish's teeth. The remora hitchhikes rides on sharks, rays, whales, and other sea creatures. Using a sucker on top of its head, a remora attaches itself to a host. The remora benefits from the easy access to food, using its protruding jaw to collect both scraps dropped by its host and parasites it scrapes from the host's body.

Offering a similar service on land are several types of birds. The rhinoceros bird, for example, will perch on the back of the rhinoceros to eat the swarms of annoying insects that continually torment the rhinoceros.

15. A Sound Environment

12 errors—2 content; 5 grammar; 2 punctuation; 1 spelling; 2 usage

A Sound Environment Errors

Boom bah dah boom! I love studying to the beat of the latest tune, but as Mahmoud and me[1] were doing our science lesson, my song was interrupted by the smoke alarm. (Can you believe it was set off by Dad's "cooking?[2]") I again picked up the beat as we resumed our lesson on sound.

We read that sound is created when an object vibrates. When a tuning fork is struck, the prongs vibrate back and forth, pushing and pulling on the surrounding air and causing waves. By vibrating slowly, a large tuning fork makes sound waves of low *frequency*. Smaller tuning forks make sound waves of higher frequency because they[3] vibrate more rapidly. Frequency is measured in cycles per second (cps).

"Whose[4] playing the piano?" Mahmoud asked suddenly. My mom had hit the highest note[5] having a frequency of 1500[6] cycles per second. Mahmoud could certainly hear it better than me[7] (I had to strain!).

Next, we learned how sounds can differ in *amplitude*, or loudness. The distance the prongs of the tuning fork move back and forth determines amplitude. The affect[8] of a small amount of movement is a quiet sound. The greater the distance the prongs move, the greater the displacement of air and the louder the sound. We compared illustrations in our text. The two graphs showed tones of the same frequency; however, the wave in the second graph represented a quieter[9] tone.

Far above, a jet broke the sound barrier. Vaguely aware of it, I thought, "If that sound was[10] any softer, I wouldn't hear it at all." Mahmoud, however, was exasperated. "Who can study here?" he ranted. "If I would have[11] known there would be so much noise, I would have studied sound at home, where it's quiet!" Was he inferring[12] that my home was not?

1. *I*—Grammar: pronoun used as subject of adverb clause **[3.22]**
2. *"cooking"?*)—Punctuation: question mark outside quotation marks when it doesn't apply to quoted material **[5.59]**
3. *A smaller tuning fork makes* sound waves of higher frequency because *it vibrates*—Grammar: ambiguous pronoun reference **[3.19]** (Acceptable: because *smaller tuning forks* vibrate)
4. *"Who's*—Spelling **[6.1]**
5. *note,* having—Punctuation: comma used with nonessential participial phrase **[5.31]**
6. *15,000*—Content: see caption **[2.1]**
7. better than *I*—Grammar: pronoun following *than* in incomplete construction (verb implied—better than I could hear) **[3.24]**
8. *effect*—Usage: word pair (effect/affect) **[4.18]**
9. *louder*—Content: see illustration **[2.1]** (Acceptable: a *tone of greater amplitude*. OR wave in the *first* graph represented a quieter tone.)
10. *were*—Grammar: subjunctive mood used in contrary-to-fact statement **[3.32]** (Acceptable: sound *had been* any…wouldn't *have heard* it)
11. If I *had* known—Grammar: avoid *would have* in *if* clause (use past perfect tense) **[3.31]**
12. *implying*—Usage: word pair (imply/infer) **[4.18]**

A Sound Environment Corrected

Boom bah dah boom! I love studying to the beat of the latest tune, but as Mahmoud and I were doing our science lesson, my song was interrupted by the smoke alarm. (Can you believe it was set off by Dad's "cooking"?) I again picked up the beat as we resumed our lesson on sound.

We read that sound is created when an object vibrates. When a tuning fork is struck, the prongs vibrate back and forth, pushing and pulling on the surrounding air and causing waves. By vibrating slowly, a large tuning fork makes sound waves of low *frequency*. A smaller tuning fork makes sound waves of higher frequency because it vibrates more rapidly. Frequency is measured in cycles per second (cps).

"Who's playing the piano?" Mahmoud asked suddenly. My mom had hit the highest note, having a frequency of 15,000 cycles per second. Mahmoud could certainly hear it better than I (I had to strain!).

Next, we learned how sounds can differ in *amplitude*, or loudness. The distance the prongs of the tuning fork move back and forth determines amplitude. The effect of a small amount of movement is a quiet sound. The greater the distance the prongs move, the greater the displacement of air and the louder the sound. We compared illustrations in our text. The two graphs showed tones of the same frequency; however, the wave in the second graph represented a louder tone.

Far above, a jet broke the sound barrier. Vaguely aware of it, I thought, "If that sound were any softer, I wouldn't hear it at all." Mahmoud, however, was exasperated. "Who can study here?" he ranted. "If I had known there would be so much noise, I would have studied sound at home, where it's quiet!" Was he implying that my home was not?

16. A Contest of Wills

16 errors—3 content; 2 capitalization;
3 grammar; 4 punctuation; 1 spelling; 3 usage

A Contest of Wills Errors

Bedecked in traditional viking[1] armor.[2] Willi Olson proudly guided her Morgan horse in the biannual[3] Heritage Parade. She had glued the horns on her helmet and had made the shield, having [4]an octet of[4] peripheral circles, from a shiny hub-cap. A heritage parade offered the perfect arena for her busting[5] ethnic pride. Now William Lucido, behind who[6] she rode, challenged that pride.

"My ancestors[7] conquests were much greater than yours," he boasted. "Why, the Roman acquisitions were immense—"

"Oh yeah?[8] Willi interrupted. "They weren't so great. The Vikings were superlative seafarers! They reached north[9] America long before Columbus—"

As the retorts flew, Willi leaned farther and farther toward her opponent[10] her heavy weapon swinging precariously. Before she knew it, Willi has[11] slid out of her saddle and was sprawling on the parade ground as[12] a ragdoll. William laughed so hard that he fell out of his chariot. His fall, in turn, set off Willi's laughter.

"I guess neither of us have[13] much to be proud of now!" said William, wiping the dirt off his face. Soon, the two had made up and became[14] friends.

"I guess the conquests of our ancestors aren't important," said Willi. "What really matter are the contributions we make ourselves." They applauded loudly as the planning committee announced their[15] costume contest winners[16].

1. *Viking*—Capital: proper adjective **[1.5]**
2. *armor*, Willi—Punctuation: sentence fragment (also, comma used after introductory phrase) **[5.82]**
3. *annual*—Content: see caption (yearly = annual) **[2.1]**
4. having *nine* peripheral—Content: see illustration **[2.1]**
5. *bursting*—Spelling **[6.7]**
6. *whom*—Grammar: pronoun *whom* as object **[3.26]**
7. *ancestors'*—Punctuation: apostrophe used with possessive of plural ending in *s* **[5.5]**
8. *yeah?"*—Punctuation: quotation marks enclose a direct quote **[5.60]**

9. *North*—Capital: proper noun **[1.4]**

10. *opponent,*—Punctuation: comma used with absolute phrase **[5.32]**

11. *had* slid—Grammar: helping verb (used in past perfect tense) **[3.33, 3.29]**

12. *like* a ragdoll—Usage: word pair (like/as) **[4.18]**

13. *has*—Usage: agreement of verb with indefinite pronoun (neither/has) **[4.8]**

14. *become*—Grammar: past participle (used in past perfect tense) **[3.27, 3.29]**

15. *its*—Usage: agreement of pronoun with collective subject used in singular sense (committee/its) **[4.5]**

16. *winner*—Content: see caption ("just one winner") **[2.1]**

A Contest of Wills Corrected

Bedecked in traditional Viking armor, Willi Olson proudly guided her Morgan horse in the annual Heritage Parade. She had glued the horns on her helmet and had made the shield, having nine peripheral circles, from a shiny hubcap. A heritage parade offered the perfect arena for her bursting ethnic pride. Now William Lucido, behind whom she rode, challenged that pride.

"My ancestors' conquests were much greater than yours," he boasted. "Why, the Roman acquisitions were immense—"

"Oh yeah?" Willi interrupted. "They weren't so great. The Vikings were superlative seafarers! They reached North America long before Columbus—"

As the retorts flew, Willi leaned farther and farther toward her opponent, her heavy weapon swinging precariously. Before she knew it, Willi had slid out of her saddle and was sprawling on the parade ground like a ragdoll. William laughed so hard that he fell out of his chariot. His fall, in turn, set off Willi's laughter.

"I guess neither of us has much to be proud of now!" said William, wiping the dirt off his face. Soon, the two had made up and become friends.

"I guess the conquests of our ancestors aren't important," said Willi. "What really matter are the contributions we make ourselves." They applauded loudly as the planning committee announced its costume contest winner.

17. Virtually Real

13 errors—2 content; 1 grammar; 6 punctuation; 1 spelling; 3 usage

Virtually Real Errors

"I'm slipping off the rock ledge. I-I don't think I can hold on anymore!" you shout as you grope wildly for a jutting stone—anything—that might prolong your tentative hold on the cliff's face. Up and down,[1] runs the sheer rock wall to which you are plastered. You can hardly contain you're[2] terror,[3] because you are looking straight down into a mile-deep canyon. You've had enough. With shaking hands, [4]your headgear tears off[4] to find yourself in the security of your own living room.

The canyon "exists"[5] in the memory of a computer[6] not in the real world. Virtual reality programs turn photographs of scenery into three-dimensional models,[7] that you view through the tiny televisions in special headgear. Sound is also used to help simulate reality (distant "objects" are quieter than closer ones;[8]) [9]they are[9] relayed through speakers located in the handgear[10]. Wiring in special globes[11] allow[12] the computer to keep track of where you "are" in the virtual world and how you are "manipulating" any virtual objects. The computer creates a continuous presentation, which becomes the user's "world."

Since they eliminate the danger associated with training situations, virtual reality programs have shown promise in medicine, aeronautics, and engineering. They can also help whomever[13] uses them conquer the fear of high places!

1. *down* runs—Punctuation: comma unnecessary after introductory phrase immediately preceding main verb **[5.41 d]**
2. *your* terror—Spelling **[6.1]**
3. *terror* because—Punctuation: comma unnecessary when dependent clause follows main clause **[5.41 l]**
4. hands, *you tear off your headgear*—Usage: dangling modifier **[4.16]**
5. *"exists"*—Punctuation: quotation marks denote special word usage **[5.64]**
6. *computer,* not—Punctuation: commas with contrasting expressions **[5.34]**
7. *models* that you—Punctuation: comma unnecessary with essential clause **[5.41 i]**
8. *ones);*—Punctuation: semicolon outside parenthesis **[5.71]**
9. *it is*—Usage: agreement of pronoun and verb with noun (Sound/it is) **[4.2, 4.3]**
10. *headgear*—Content: see caption **[2.1]**
11. *gloves*—Content: see illustration and caption **[2.1]**
12. *allows*—Usage: agreement of verb with subject (Wiring/allows) **[4.3]**
13. *whoever*—Grammar: pronoun *whoever* as subject of noun phrase **[3.26]**

Virtually Real Corrected

"I'm slipping off the rock ledge. I-I don't think I can hold on anymore!" you shout as you grope wildly for a jutting stone—anything—that might prolong your tentative hold on the cliff's face. Up and down runs the sheer rock wall to which you are plastered. You can hardly contain your terror because you are looking straight down into a mile-deep canyon. You've had enough. With shaking hands, you tear off your headgear to find yourself in the security of your own living room.

The canyon "exists" in the memory of a computer, not in the real world. Virtual reality programs turn photographs of scenery into three-dimensional models that you view through the tiny televisions in special headgear. Sound is also used to help simulate reality (distant "objects" are quieter than closer ones); it is relayed through speakers located in the headgear. Wiring in special gloves allows the computer to keep track of where you "are" in the virtual world and how you are "manipulating" any virtual objects. The computer creates a continuous presentation, which becomes the user's "world."

Since they eliminate the dangers associated with training situations, virtual reality programs have shown promise in medicine, aeronautics, and engineering. They can also help whoever uses them conquer the fear of high places!

18. A Unique Mammal

14 errors—2 content; 3 grammar; 8 punctuation; 4 usage

A Unique Mammal Errors

The platypus is one of only two egg[1] laying mammals. (The other is the spiny anteater, or echidna.) The platypus is a monotreme, a mammalian order distinct from the marsupials and placentals.

The platypus inhibits[2] a variety of waterways;[3] streams, rivers, lakes, and ponds. It feeds primarily on small animals (shellfish, worms, insects[4] and water plants that it finds,[5] when it dives to the waters[6] bottom. Unlike other mammals living in or near water, the platypus cannot dive for very long,[7] it stays underwater for about an hour[8].

The platypus lives in a burrow [9]near the water in a bank[9]. The female digs the burrow, which may be up to 50 feet long, and makes a nest of moist leaves for her eggs. She lies[10] from 1 to 3 eggs, which have soft[11] leathery shells like those of reptiles. The female incubates the eggs until they hatch, about 10 days. During this time[12] the female keeps the opening to the burrow plugged.

Newborn platypuses are hairy[13] and about one inch long. Like all female mammals, the mother platypus has mammary glands that secrete milk. Holding the tiny platypuses against her body with her tail, [14]they nurse[14]. It is several months before the young platypuses leave their burrow for the first time.

1. *egg-laying*—Punctuation: hyphen used in compound adjective **[5.48]**

2. *inhabits*—Usage: word pair (inhabit/inhibit) **[4.18]**

3. *waterways:* streams—Punctuation: colon introduces a list of items **[5.10]**

4. *insects)*—Punctuation: parentheses used (in pairs) to enclose supplementary words **[5.49]**

5. *finds* when—Punctuation: comma unnecessary with essential clause **[5.41 i]**

6. *water's* bottom—Punctuation: *'s* used with singular possessive **[5.4]**

7. *long;* it—Punctuation: semicolon separates main clauses joined without coordinating conjunction (corrects comma splice) **[5.68]**

8. about *a minute.*—Content: see caption **[2.1]**
   (Acceptable: about *60 seconds*)

9. lives in a burrow *in a bank near the water*—Usage: misplaced modifier **[4.15]**

10. She *lays*—Usage: word pair (lay/lie) **[4.18]**

11. *soft,* leathery shells—Punctuation: comma separates coordinate adjectives **[5.24]**

12. this *time,* the—Punctuation: comma used after introductory phrase **[5.26]**

13. *hairless*—Content: see caption **[2.1]**

14. Holding the tiny platypuses...with her tail, *the female nurses them*—Usage: dangling modifier **[4.16]**

A Unique Mammal Corrected

The platypus is one of only two egg-laying mammals. (The other is the spiny anteater, or echidna.) The platypus is a monotreme, a mammalian order distinct from the marsupials and placentals.

The platypus inhabits a variety of waterways: streams, rivers, lakes, and ponds. It feeds primarily on small animals (shellfish, worms, insects) and water plants that it finds when it dives to the water's bottom. Unlike other mammals living in or near water, the platypus cannot dive for very long; it stays underwater for about a minute.

The platypus lives in a burrow in a bank near the water. The female digs the burrow, which may be up to 50 feet long, and makes a nest of moist leaves for her eggs. She lays from 1 to 3 eggs, which have soft, leathery shells like those of reptiles. The female incubates the eggs until they hatch, about 10 days. During this time, the female keeps the opening to the burrow plugged.

Newborn platypuses are hairless and about one inch long. Like all female mammals, the mother platypus has mammary glands that secrete milk. Holding the tiny platypuses against her body with her tail, the female nurses them. It is several months before the young platypuses leave their burrow for the first time.

19. It's a Zoo Out There

17 errors—1 content; 2 grammar; 8 punctuation; 6 usage

It's a Zoo Out There Errors

410 View Street
Fayetteville, AR 72702
June 16, 1994

Adam B. Fujimoto[1] Director
Cincinnati Zoo
3400 Vine Street
Cincinnati, OH 45220

Dear Mr. Fujimoto,[2]

I wish to apply for the position of nursery vet tech advertised by your institution in the June 15 issue of the *Cincinnati*

Post. Graduating in the top third of my class, [3]two years'[4] of training in animal health technology at the University of Cincinnati has been completed[3], and I am looking for a full-time position in animal care.

I admire the high caliber of the behavioral research conducted by your institution,[5] and am familiar with several of your recent articles on animal behavior;[6] "The Social Structure of the Prairie Dog Community," "The Effect of Captivity on Endangered Species",[7] and "Communication for the Species." My four[8] years[9] experience as a pet-sitter, in which I was completely responsible for the care of a diverse population of animals, give[10] me an excellent background for your current job opening. I work well with animals; there is a special bond among[11] [12]they and I[12].

I believe that I am a good match for your institution and would be very affective[13] in this.[14] I am creative, hard working, and [15]have a lot of knowledge[15] in many aspects of animal care. Please find enclosed a copy of my resume. Thank you for your consolation.[16]

Sincerely[17]

Amanda Doolittle

Amanda Doolittle

1. *Fujimoto,* Director—Punctuation: comma separates name and title **[5.20]**
2. Dear Mr. *Fujimoto:*—Punctuation: colon used after greeting of a business letter **[5.9]**
3. class, *I have completed two...Cincinnati,* and I am—Usage: dangling modifier **[4.16]**
4. two *years* of—Punctuation: unnecessary apostrophe **[5.3]**
5. *institution* and—Punctuation: comma unnecessary in compound predicate **[5.41 h]**
6. *behavior:*—Punctuation: colon introduces list of items **[5.10]**

7. Endangered *Species,"*—Punctuation: comma falls inside quotation marks **[5.40]**
8. *two* years—Content: see illustration **[2.1]**
9. *years'*—Punctuation: apostrophe used with possessive of plural **[5.5]**
10. *gives* me—Usage: agreement of verb with subject (experience/gives) **[4.3]**
11. *between*—Usage: word pair (among/between) **[4.18]**
12. *them* and *me*—Grammar: pronouns used as objects **[3.22]**
13. *effective*—Usage: word pair (affective/effective) **[4.18]**
14. this *job.*—Grammar: ambiguous pronoun reference **[3.19]**
15. and *knowledgeable* in—Usage: parallel structure **[4.11]**
16. *consideration.*—Usage: word pair (consideration/consolation) **[4.18]**
17. *Sincerely,*—Punctuation: comma used after closing of a letter **[5.21]**

It's a Zoo Out There Corrected

410 View Street
Fayetteville, AR 72702
June 16, 1994

Adam B. Fujimoto, Director
Cincinnati Zoo
3400 Vine Street
Cincinnati, OH 45220

Dear Mr. Fujimoto:

I wish to apply for the position of nursery vet tech advertised by your institution in the June 15 issue of the *Cincinnati Post.* Graduating in the top third of my class, I have completed two years of training in animal health technology at the University of Cincinnati, and I am looking for a full-time position in animal care.

I admire the high caliber of the behavioral research conducted by your institution and am familiar with several of your recent articles on animal behavior: "The Social Structure of the Prairie Dog Community," "The Effect of Captivity on

Endangered Species," and "Communication for the Species." My two years' experience as a pet-sitter, in which I was completely responsible for the care of a diverse population of animals, gives me an excellent background for your current job opening. I work well with animals; there is a special bond between them and me.

I believe that I am a good match for your institution and would be very effective in this job. I am creative, hard working, and knowledgeable in many aspects of animal care. Please find enclosed a copy of my resume. Thank you for your consideration.

Sincerely,

Amanda Doolittle

Amanda Doolittle

20. A for Ama

16 errors—2 content; 1 capitalization; 2 grammar; 8 punctuation; 1 spelling; 2 usage

A for Ama Errors

Ama is starting to panic. She wants all As[1] in geography, and the semesters[2] paper on Kenya is almost due! Born in America, Ama knows little about her ancestors' homeland; she appeals to Cousin Jomo, which[3] is very familiar with the Kenyan territory. When she asks, "Kenya[4] help me?,[5]" he gives her the following information:

- Many Kenyans speak the swahili[6] language.
- The Prime Meridian[7] divides Kenya so that it lies in both the Northern and Southern Hemispheres.
- Tourist attractions [8]both include[8] the sandy beaches of the coast and the inland animal reserves.
- On the exotic safaris, of whom[9] we hear so much, hunters are allowed to shoot only with cameras.

Jomo hopes he has been of assistance. How else can he help her.[10]

"What I really want to know is how it feels to be in Kenya?[11]" Ama says dreamily. "I'm sure the morning sun is gorgeous as it rises over the South Atlantic[12] Ocean!"

"Well, if I was[13] you," Jomo says, [14]I'd go along with Aunt Jessie when she visits our relatives this month."

"I'd love to.[15]" says Ama, waking up to reality, "but in geography, I want to get an A for 'awesome;[16]' if I were in Kenya, I'd get an F for 'far away.'"

1. *A's*—Punctuation: apostrophe used with plural of letter [5.2]
2. *semester's* paper—Punctuation: 's used with singular possessive [5.4]
3. *who*—Usage: agreement of pronoun with noun (Jomo/who) [4.2]
4. *Can you*—Spelling [6.7] (Acceptable "*Kenya*')
5. *me?*"—Punctuation: avoid multiple punctuation [5.73]
6. *Swahili* language—Capital: proper adjective [1.5]
7. The *equator*—Content: see illustration (equator divides Kenya into northern and southern portions; equator divides the earth into Northern and Southern Hemispheres) [2.1]
8. attractions *include both* the—Grammar: correlative conjunctions (both...and) each followed by parallel phrase [3.15]
9. *which*—Usage: agreement of pronoun with noun (safaris/which) [4.2]
10. *her?*—Punctuation: question mark used after direct question [5.56]
11. *Kenya,*"—Punctuation: question mark unnecessary after indirect question (comma separates quote from speaker) [5.57]
12. *Indian* Ocean—Content: see illustration (the sun rises in the east; the Indian Ocean is to Kenya's east) [2.1]
13. *were*—Grammar: subjunctive mood used in contrary-to-fact statement [3.32]
14. "*I'd*—Punctuation: quotation marks

enclose both parts of divided quotation **[5.60]**

15. *to,"*—Punctuation: comma separates quote from speaker **[5.39]**

16. *'awesome';*—Punctuation: semicolon falls outside quotation mark **[5.72]**

A for Ama Corrected

Ama is starting to panic. She wants all A's in geography, and the semester's paper on Kenya is almost due! Born in America, Ama knows little about her ancestors' homeland; she appeals to Cousin Jomo, who is very familiar with the Kenyan territory. When she asks, "Can you help me?" he gives her the following information:

- Many Kenyans speak the Swahili language.
- The equator divides Kenya so that it lies in both the Northern and Southern Hemispheres.
- Tourist attractions include both the sandy beaches of the coast and the inland animal reserves.
- On the exotic safaris, of which we hear so much, hunters are allowed to shoot only with cameras.

Jomo hopes he has been of assistance. How else can he help her?

"What I really want to know is how it feels to be in Kenya," Ama says dreamily. "I'm sure the morning sun is gorgeous as it rises over the Indian Ocean!"

"Well, if I were you," Jomo says, "I'd go along with Aunt Jessie when she visits our relatives this month."

"I'd love to," says Ama, waking up to reality, "but in geography, I want to get an A for 'awesome'; if I were in Kenya, I'd get an F for 'far away.'"

21. Something Old, Something New

15 errors—3 content; 2 grammar; 6 punctuation; 1 spelling; 3 usage

Something Old, Something New Errors

What really happens to the bottles and cans we recycle daily?.[1] The technology of recycling has expand[2] tremendously as scientists [3]not only learn[3] to remake the same products from old ones but also to create entirely new products. Used glass bottles can be melted down and turned into new bottles or into fiberglass insulation. Clear plastic bottles can be recycled into new bottles (not used for food), or it[4] can end up as the stuffing in a sleeping bag (fiberfill!)[5]

The three basic steps to recycling materials include:[6] sorting the recyclable materials from the waste, processing the sorted materials into raw materials, and to make[7] new products from these raw materials[8] Recycling glass requires an additional step. The glass must be sorted by weight[9] before it is processed,[10] if colored and clear glass are melted together, they produce a muddy brown glass that most manafacturers[11] find unacceptable for their products.

Once separated[12], magnets are used to remove any metal caps or lids. Then the glass is crushed, and paper labels are removed by suction. The resulting crushed glass, called cullet, is mixed with sand and melted in a glass furnace. The melted glass can then be molded into new containers or spun into fiberglass insulation.

Glass is an excellent material for recycling,[13] because, like metal, it can be melted down and reused over and over again. When we compare the proportions of materials that consumers recycle, glass ranks second[14]; about 22% of the glass thrown away is recycled, compared to about 10%[15] of plastic.

1. *daily? The*—Punctuation: avoid multiple punctuation **[5.73]**

2. has *expanded*—Grammar: past participle (used in present perfect tense) **[3.27, 3.29]**

3. *learn not only* to—Grammar: correlative conjunctions (not only...but also) each followed by parallel phrase **[3.15]**

(Acceptable though meaning changes slightly: *not only learn...but also create*)

4. *they* can—Usage: agreement of pronoun with noun **[4.2]**

5. *fiberfill)!*—Punctuation: exclamation point outside parenthesis **[5.46]**

6. *include* sorting—Punctuation: colon unnecessary (OR colon must be preceded by independent clause) **[5.13]** (Acceptable: include *the following*:)

7. and *making* new products—Usage: parallel structure (gerund) **[4.11, 3.38]**

8. *materials.* Recycling—Punctuation: period after declarative sentence **[5.52]**

9. by *color*—Content: see caption **[2.1]**

10. *processed;* if colored—Punctuation: semicolon used to separate main clauses joined without coordinating conjunction (corrects comma splice) **[5.68]**

11. *manufacturers*—Spelling **[6.7]**

12. Once *the glass is* separated—Usage: dangling modifier **[4.16]**

13. *recycling* because—Punctuation: comma unnecessary when dependent clause follows main clause **[5.41 l]**

14. *third*—Content: see graph **[2.1]**

15. *5% of plastic*—Content: see graph **[2.1]**

Something Old, Something New Corrected

What really happens to the bottles and cans we recycle daily? The technology of recycling has expanded tremendously as scientists learn not only to remake the same products from old ones but also to create entirely new products. Used glass bottles can be melted down and turned into new bottles or into fiberglass insulation. Clear plastic bottles can be recycled into new bottles (not used for food), or they can end up as the stuffing in a sleeping bag (fiberfill)!

The three basic steps to recycling materials include sorting the recyclable materials from the waste, processing the sorted materials into raw materials, and making new products from these raw materials. Recycling glass requires an additional step. The glass must be sorted by color before it is processed; if colored and clear glass are melted together, they produce a muddy brown glass that most manufacturers find unacceptable for their products.

Once the glass is separated, magnets are used to remove any metal caps or lids. Then the glass is crushed, and paper labels are removed by suction. The resulting crushed glass, called cullet, is mixed with sand and melted in a glass furnace. The melted glass can then be molded into new containers or spun into fiberglass insulation.

Glass is an excellent material for recycling because, like metal, it can be melted down and reused over and over again. When we compare the proportions of materials that consumers recycle, glass ranks third; about 22% of the glass thrown away is recycled, compared to about 5% of plastic.

22. All Washed Up

17 errors—2 content; 4 grammar; 8 punctuation; 3 usage

All Washed Up Errors

At his Friday night liars' club, Gerald Smith recites the following anecdote about the flood of [1]89.

"It was almost bedtime for Amos and I[2], but I was doing the wash. Amos gave me a warning (he loved playing [3]Dad':[4]) [5]The automatic cutoff is broken, so be sure to turn the water off. I wouldn't want it to overflow!' Amos didn't notice the storm brewing as he went off to his bed in the loft." [6]

"I guess it wasn't[7] scarcely an hour later that the floodwaters begun[8] to rise, and the rain continued all night as we slept. I was the first to awaken,[9] and hear on the radio that homes were being evacuated by helicopter. As the water level approached are[10] loft, I shouted at Amos and scrambled through the trap door to the log[11] roof, hoping to flag down the rescuers. Amos followed me, half asleep. Before I could get him into the chopper, he groused, 'If you would have[12] only listened to me, this disaster wouldn't have happened.' The winds were whipping us left and right, and I was afraid we'd been[13] tossed into the river and swept toward the pine tree[14] downstream.

"[15]Don't be a fool!' I shouted eagerly[16]. 'Just get into the helicopter before we drown!' We finally settled into the chopper and were carried to safety.

"Even though we survived that fiasco without a scratch, to this day Amos refuses to own a washing machine.[17]

1. '89—Punctuation: apostrophe replaces numerals in year [5.1]
2. Amos and *me*—Grammar: pronoun used as object [3.22]
3. *'Dad'*—Punctuation: quotation marks denote special word usage (single quotation marks within quote) [5.64, 5.65]
4. *'Dad'):*—Punctuation: colon used outside parenthesis [5.14]
5. *'The*—Punctuation: single quotation marks enclose quote within quote [5.65]
6. *loft.*—Punctuation: quotation marks unnecessary at end of paragraph (except last) for quote spanning several paragraphs [5.62]
7. *was* scarcely—Usage: double negative [4.19]
   (Acceptable: *wasn't an* hour)
8. *began*—Grammar: past tense (irregular) [3.29]
9. *awaken* and—Punctuation: comma unnecessary in compound predicate [5.41 h]
10. *our*—Usage: word pair (are/our) [4.18]

11. *shingled* roof—Content: see illustration [2.1]
    (Acceptable: to *the roof*)
12. you *had* only—Grammar: avoid *would have* in *if* clause (use past perfect tense) [3.31]
13. we'd *be*—Grammar: infinitive [3.27]
14. toward the *tower*—Content: see illustration and caption (from the men, water flows toward the tower, not the pine) [2.1]
    (Acceptable: swept *downstream.*)
15. *"Don't*—Punctuation: single quotation marks enclose quote within quote [5.65]
16. *anxiously*—Usage: word pair (eager/anxious) [4.18]
17. *machine."*—Punctuation: quotation marks enclose a direct quote (final paragraph of quote spanning several paragraphs) [5.62]

All Washed Up Corrected

At his Friday night liars' club, Gerald Smith recites the following anecdote about the flood of '89.

"It was almost bedtime for Amos and me, but I was doing the wash. Amos gave me a warning (he loved playing 'Dad'): 'The automatic cutoff is broken, so be sure to turn the water off. I wouldn't want it to overflow!' Amos didn't notice the storm brewing as he went off to his bed in the loft.

"I guess it was scarcely an hour later that the floodwaters began to rise, and the rain continued all night as we slept. I was the first to awaken and hear on the radio that homes were being evacuated by helicopter. As the water level approached our loft, I shouted at Amos and scrambled through the trap door to the shingled roof, hoping to flag down the rescuers. Amos followed me, half asleep. Before I could get him into the chopper, he groused, 'If you had only listened to me, this disaster wouldn't have happened.' The winds were whipping us left and right, and I was afraid we'd be tossed into the river and swept toward the tower downstream.

"'Don't be a fool!' I shouted anxiously. 'Just get into the helicopter before we drown!' We finally settled into the chopper and were carried to safety.

"Even though we survived that fiasco without a scratch, to this day Amos refuses to own a washing machine."

23. Recipe for Destruction

14 errors—4 content; 2 capitalization;
2 grammar; 4 punctuation; 1 spelling; 1 usage

Recipe for Destruction Errors

The powerful, violent wind storms known as tornadoes are found in areas where large masses of rapidly moving cold, dry air overrun warm[1] humid air. In the United States, this condition occurs most frequently in the southwest[2, 3] and the south[3] during the [4]Spring and early Summer[4].

When a cold front overruns a warm front.[5] The warm air rises and the cold air descends. Large masses of rapidly rising warm, humid air (updrafts) form cumulonimbus clouds (thunderclouds). Cumulonimbus clouds reach high into the stratosphere where the air in the warm updrafts cools and descends,[6] the resulting downdrafts carry rain.

The strong downdrafts[7] in the thundercloud is[8] the first ingredient in forming a tornado. The second requirement is for the air too[9] start rotating. This[10] occurs when a crosswind creates a shear that cuts through the cumulus[11] cloud. The shear blows past the warm updrafts, make[12] the air spiral,[13] as this warm air spins faster, the spiral tightens and draws in more warm air. Eventually, a whirlpool shape is formed with spiraling updrafts surrounding an increasingly strong downdraft. The funnel of this whirlpool shape begins stretching down out of the cloud. When the funnel cloud reaches the ground, it

can contain winds moving at more than 3000[14] miles per hour!

1. *warm,* humid—Punctuation: comma separates coordinate adjectives **[5.24]** (Acceptable: warm *and* humid)
2. *Midwest*—Content: see illustration **[2.1]**
3. *Midwest* and the *South*—Capital: direction used as proper geographic name **[1.6]**
4. *spring* and *early summer*—Capital: unnecessary in season (unless personified) **[1.12]**
5. *front, the*—Punctuation: sentence fragment **[5.82]**
6. *descends;* the—Punctuation: semicolon separates main clauses joined without coordinating conjunction (corrects comma splice) **[5.68]** (Acceptable: *descends and*)
7. *updrafts*—Content: see caption **[2.1]**
8. updrafts...*are*—Usage: agreement of verb with subject **[4.3]**
9. *to* start—Spelling **[6.1]**
10. This *rotation*—Grammar: general pronoun reference **[3.19]**
11. *cumulonimbus*—Content: see caption **[2.1]**
12. *making* the—Grammar: verbal (participle as adjective) **[3.37]**
13. *spiral;* as—Punctuation: semicolon separates main clauses joined without coordinating conjunction (corrects comma splice) **[5.68]**
14. *300* miles—Content: see caption **[2.1]**

Recipe for Destruction Corrected

The powerful, violent wind storms known as tornadoes are found in areas where large masses of rapidly moving cold, dry air overrun warm, humid air. In the United States, this condition occurs most frequently in the Midwest and the South during the spring and early summer.

When a cold front overruns a warm front, the warm air rises and the cold air descends. Large masses of rapidly rising warm, humid air (updrafts) form cumulonimbus clouds (thunderclouds). Cumulonimbus clouds reach high into the stratosphere where the air in the warm updrafts cools and descends; the resulting downdrafts carry rain.

The strong updrafts in the thundercloud are the first ingredient in forming a tornado. The second requirement is for the air to start rotating. This rotation occurs when a crosswind creates a shear that cuts through the cumulonimbus cloud. The shear blows past the warm updrafts, making the air spiral; as this warm air spins faster, the spiral tightens and draws in more warm air. Eventually, a whirlpool shape is formed with spiraling updrafts surrounding an increasingly strong downdraft. The funnel of this whirlpool shape begins stretching down out of the cloud. When the funnel cloud reaches the ground, it can contain winds moving at more than 300 miles per hour!

24. Placid Thrills

16 errors—2 content; 1 capitalization; 4 grammar; 4 punctuation; 5 usage

Placid Thrills Errors

What a surprise I'll have for Robert on Christmas day[1]! By then, we will[2] flown to the Lake Placid, N.J[3].[4] Olympic grounds, site of the 1922[5] and 1980 winter games. During the off-Olympic years, regular folks like ourselves[6] can experience the thrill of winter events on a real Olympic course. When I bring[7] Robert to Lake Placid, he will have a blast!

Thrill seekers may take part in any of the following (if they dare:[8]) luge, skiing, skating, tobogganing, dogsledding, bobsledding, snowmobiling, and sleigh riding. (I almost wish there were less[9] events to choose from! The dogsledding or snowmobiling take[10] too long for Robert and I[11], but we may briefly watch a team

of dogs pulling a sled[12] and ice skaters on the rink.)

The high point of the trip will be Robert's favorite event: the fast and sometimes dangerous sport of mens'[13] bobsledding. A four-man bobsledding team all works[14] together in synchronization. One drives, one brakes, and the other two bob rhythmically as the sled careens down icy slopes at speeds up to 90 miles per hour. Sharp turns and a set of banked walls helps[15] to control the sled, keeping it on course. By the time we leave Lake Placid, Robert will take[16] the most thrilling ride of his life and will be a true "Bob"sledder! He will never forget his Olympic surprise of a lifetime.

1. *Day*—Capital: holiday **[1.11]**
2. will *have* flown—Grammar: helping verb (used in future perfect tense) **[3.33]**
   (Acceptable: will *be* flying)
3. *N.Y.*—Content: see caption **[2.1]**
4. *N.Y.,*—Punctuation: comma used after state (city, state,) in a sentence **[5.15]**
5. *1932*—Content: see caption **[2.1]**
6. *us*—Grammar: pronoun used as object (not reflexive) **[3.26]**
7. *take*—Usage: word pair (bring/take) **[4.18]**
8. *dare):*—Punctuation: colon used outside parenthesis **[5.14]**
9. *fewer*—Usage: word pair (less/fewer) **[4.18]**
10. *takes*—Usage: agreement of verb with closer of two subjects joined by *or* **[4.6]**
11. *me*—Grammar: pronoun used as object **[3.26]**
12. *sled,*—Punctuation: comma used to avoid ambiguity **[5.36]**
13. *men's*—Punctuation: 's after possessive of plural not ending in *s* **[5.6]**
14. team all *work*—Usage: agreement of verb with collective subject used in plural sense **[4.4]**
15. *help*—Usage: agreement of verb with two subjects joined by *and* **[4.6]**

16. will *have taken*—Grammar: context of article requires future perfect tense (by the time he leaves, Robert will already have taken the ride) **[3.29]**

Placid Thrills Corrected

What a surprise I'll have for Robert on Christmas Day! By then, we will have flown to the Lake Placid, N.Y., Olympic grounds, site of the 1932 and 1980 winter games. During the off-Olympic years, regular folks like us can experience the thrill of winter events on a real Olympic course. When I take Robert to Lake Placid, he will have a blast!

Thrill seekers may take part in any of the following (if they dare): luge, skiing, skating, tobogganing, dogsledding, bobsledding, snowmobiling, and sleigh riding. (I almost wish there were fewer events to choose from! The dogsledding or snowmobiling takes too long for Robert and me, but we may briefly watch a team of dogs pulling a sled, and ice skaters on the rink.)

The high point of the trip will be Robert's favorite event: the fast and sometimes dangerous sport of men's bobsledding. A four-man bobsledding team all work together in synchronization. One drives, one brakes, and the other two bob rhythmically as the sled careens down icy slopes at speeds up to 90 miles per hour. Sharp turns and a set of banked walls help to control the sled, keeping it on course. By the time we leave Lake Placid, Robert will have taken the most thrilling ride of his life and will be a true "Bob"sledder! He will never forget his Olympic surprise of a lifetime.

25. Stalk Your Claim

16 errors—2 content; 2 grammar; 9 punctuation; 2 spelling; 1 usage

Stalk Your Claim Errors

It is 4:30 at Prouse's, and the last of the four o[1]clock crowd had[2] now disap-

peared into the storm. Gerry Sadowski's story, [3]Count Ragula,[3] is doing well as a thriller, and she is pleased with the signing turnout. Suddenly, the lights dim. Hands trembling[4] Gerry signs an extra copy of her book. She is unaware of the dark shape (so like *Wicked Places'* main character)![5] moving stealthily towards her. A shadow crosses the page as she crosses her t[6]s. She looks up. Her eyes pop, but her scream is cut off.

"I'm sorry to disturb you, Miss Scott," says John Aziz. With a sweep of his tattered cape (he has dressed in costume to convince the author of his enthusiasm[7], he opens his arms imploringly. "Would you be kind enough to advise me on publishing some work of my own"?[8]

The store lights brighten as Gerry sighs with relief. "I-I'd be glad to," she stammers, still a little flustered. She gains momentum. "You must sink your teeth into your work. The principle[9] key to success is dedication, so if I was[10] you, I'd go to the writers' class I'm teaching next week. I'll be here only 15[11] minutes more, but if you show up for [12]"Writers Which[13] Write,"[12] I'll teach you to inject excitement into the lifeblood of your project."

"Alright[14]!" John exclaims. Out in the storm, he congratulates himself. "Today, I have found a mentor by capitalizing on [15]Friday the 13th[15]; next month, I will learn the 'Write' way to publish my how-to article, 'Opportunity Stalks'.[16]"

1. *o'clock*—Punctuation: apostrophe used with contraction **[5.1]**
2. *has* now disappeared—Grammar: helping verb (used in present perfect tense) **[3.33]**
   (Acceptable: crowd *have* now disappeared)
3. *"Count Ragula,"*—Punctuation: quotation marks enclose story title **[5.63]**
4. *trembling,* Gerry—Punctuation: comma used with absolute phrase **[5.32]**

5. *character!)*—Punctuation: parenthetical exclamation [5.51]
(Acceptable: delete exclamation point)

6. *t's*—Punctuation: apostrophe used with plural of letter [5.2]

7. *enthusiasm),*—Punctuation: parentheses used (in pairs) to enclose supplementary words [5.49]

8. *own?"*—Punctuation: quoted question [5.58]

9. *principal*—Spelling [6.1]

10. if I *were*—Grammar: subjunctive mood used in contrary-to-fact statement [3.32]

11. *30* minutes—Content: see illustration and caption [2.1]
(Acceptable: *half an hour*)

12. *'Writers…Write,'*—Punctuation: single quotation marks used within quote [5.65]

13. *'Writers Who*—Usage: agreement of pronoun with noun [4.2]

14. *"All right!"*—Spelling [6.6]

15. capitalizing on *Halloween*—Content: see illustration (October 31 is Halloween) [2.1]
(Acceptable: *October 31st*)

16. *Stalks.'"*—Punctuation: period inside quotation marks (both sets) [5.54]

Stalk Your Claim Corrected

It is 4:30 at Prouse's, and the last of the four o'clock crowd has now disappeared into the storm. Gerry Sadowski's story, "Count Ragula," is doing well as a thriller, and she is pleased with the signing turnout. Suddenly, the lights dim. Hands trembling, Gerry signs an extra copy of her book. She is unaware of the dark shape (so like *Wicked Places'* main character!) moving stealthily towards her. A shadow crosses the page as she crosses her t's. She looks up. Her eyes pop, but her scream is cut off.

"I'm sorry to disturb you, Miss Scott," says John Aziz. With a sweep of his tattered cape (he has dressed in costume to convince the author of his enthusiasm), he opens his arms imploringly. "Would you be kind enough to advise me on publishing some work of my own?"

The store lights brighten as Gerry sighs with relief. "I-I'd be glad to," she stammers, still a little flustered. She gains momentum. "You must sink your teeth into your work. The principal key to success is dedication, so if I were you, I'd go to the writers' class I'm teaching next week. I'll be here only 30 minutes more, but if you show up for 'Writers Who Write,' I'll teach you to inject excitement into the lifeblood of your project."

"All right!" John exclaims. Out in the storm, he congratulates himself. "Today, I have found a mentor by capitalizing on Halloween; next month, I will learn the 'Write' way to publish my how-to article, 'Opportunity Stalks.'"

26. Double Take

16 errors—3 content; 1 capitalization; 4 grammar; 3 punctuation; 2 spelling; 3 usage

Double Take Errors

As we were driving past Anderson Slough yesterday, we saw alot[1] of commotion on the old bridge. The bridge had been abandoned for months[2] yet there were several cars and trucks on it.

As a pickup neared the center of the bridge, the boards[3] with a deafening crack gave way[3]. We watched in horror as the car[4] fell abruptly into the slough, ending up only partial[5] immersed because it was high[6] tide.

The driver climbed out though[7] a window and clung to a nearby python[8]. We raced towards the bridge to see if we could help. As we ran onto the bridge, someone yelled[9] "cut[10], cut!" Looking around, [11]there were several pieces of equipment along the shore. We had stumbled onto the set of a movie,[12] and had almost taken on starring roles!

The crew was[13] busy yelling directions

to each other, so we stop[14] to quietly watch[15] as they proceeded to film the driver's rescue. If we [16]would have known about the film, we would have dressed for the occasion!

1. *a lot*—Spelling **[6.6]**
2. *months,* yet—Punctuation: comma used before coordinating conjunction joining independent clauses **[5.37]**
3. *gave way with a deafening crack*—Usage: misplaced modifier **[4.15]**
4. *truck*—Content: see illustration and caption **[2.1]**
5. *partially*—Grammar: adverb modifies verb **[3.4]**
6. *low* tide—Content: see illustration (high tide marks on the pylons are far above present water level) **[2.1]**
7. *through*—Spelling **[6.7]**
8. a nearby *pylon*—Content: see caption and illustration **[2.1]**
9. *yelled,*—Punctuation: comma separates quote from speaker **[5.39]**
10. *"Cut,* cut!"—Capital: first word in quotation **[1.2]**
11. around, *we saw* several—Usage: dangling modifier **[4.16]**
12. *movie* and had—Punctuation: comma unnecessary in compound predicate **[5.41 h]**
13. The crew *were* busy—Usage: agreement of verb with collective subject used in plural sense **[4.4]**
14. *stopped*—Grammar: past tense **[3.29]**
15. to *watch* quietly—Grammar: don't split infinitive **[3.40]**
16. If we *had* known—Grammar: avoid *would have* in *if* clause (use past perfect tense) **[3.31]**

Double Take Corrected

As we were driving past Anderson Slough yesterday, we saw a lot of commotion on the old bridge. The bridge had been abandoned for months, yet there were several cars and trucks on it.

As a pickup neared the center of the bridge, the boards gave way with a deaf-

ening crack. We watched in horror as the truck fell abruptly into the slough, ending up only partially immersed because it was low tide.

The driver climbed out through a window and clung to a nearby pylon. We raced towards the bridge to see if we could help. As we ran onto the bridge, someone yelled, "Cut, cut!" Looking around, we saw several pieces of equipment along the shore. We had stumbled onto the set of a movie and had almost taken on starring roles!

The crew were busy yelling directions to each other, so we stopped to watch quietly as they proceeded to film the driver's rescue. If we had known about the film, we would have dressed for the occasion!

27. Granting Health

16 errors—2 content; 1 capitalization; 8 punctuation; 3 spelling; 2 usage

Granting Health Errors

August 15, 1993
Dr. Gloria Lin[1] Director
American Geriatric[2] Association
113 Ringwood Drive
Houston, TX,[3] 77111

Dear dr[4]. Lin,[5]

No one wants too[6] see a child die of a heart attack. The St. George Institute is leading the fight against cholesterol disorders that can claim young lives.

Although some forms of cholesterol disorders can be treated with diet and drugs[7] the lethal form of familial hypercholesterolemia is a more serious phenomena[8]. Mutated genes produce an abnormal form of the low-density-lipoprotein (LDL) receptor. The liver is rendered incapable of removing LDL from the blood. As a result, patients as young as ten years old develop arteriosclerosis, which can lead to fatal heart attacks and strokes.

Thanks to your June,[9] [10]92 grant of $50,000, our team were[11] able to complete research that enabled us to provide gene therapy to three patients. The results bode well for more widespread treatment. In fact[12] with your grant of $300,000[13], the St. George Institute of Molecular Research could extend its treatment capabilities to the international community.

The accompanying application details the research, procedures, and follow-up activities that we have implemented. Two independent analysis[14] of our plans for facilities expansion, as well as the projected increase in treatment capability, is[15] included. The enclosed vitae list the backgrounds and past experience of my clinical team.

Your consideration is greatly appreciated.

Sincerely;[16]

Claudia A. Jackson

Claudia A. Jackson, Ph.D.

1. *Lin,* Director—Punctuation: comma separates name and title [5.20]
2. *Genetic*—Content: see caption [2.1]
3. *TX* 77111—Punctuation: comma unnecessary before ZIP code [5.15]
4. *Dr.* Lin—Capital: title used as part of name [1.8]
5. *Lin:*—Punctuation: colon after greeting of a business letter [5.9]
6. *to*—Spelling [6.1]
7. *drugs,*—Punctuation: comma with introductory dependent clause [5.26]
8. *phenomenon*—Spelling (singular) [6.5]
9. *June* '92—Punctuation: comma unnecessary between month and year [5.41 a]
10. *'92*—Punctuation: apostrophe replaces numerals in year [5.1]
11. team *was*—Usage: agreement of verb with collective subject used in singular sense [4.4]
12. *fact,*—Punctuation: comma used after introductory words [5.26]
13. *$500,000*—Content: see caption [2.1]
14. *analyses*—Spelling (plural) [6.5]
15. *are*—Usage: agreement of verb with subject (analyses/are) [4.3]
16. *Sincerely,*—Punctuation: comma used after closing of a letter [5.21]

Granting Health Corrected

August 15, 1993
Dr. Gloria Lin, Director
American Genetic Association
113 Ringwood Drive
Houston, TX 77111

Dear Dr. Lin:

No one wants to see a child die of a heart attack. The St. George Institute is leading the fight against cholesterol disorders that can claim young lives.

Although some forms of cholesterol disorders can be treated with diet and drugs, the lethal form of familial hypercholesterolemia is a more serious phenomenon. Mutated genes produce an abnormal form of the low-density-lipoprotein (LDL) receptor. The liver is rendered incapable of removing LDL from the blood. As a result, patients as young as ten years old develop arteriosclerosis, which can lead to fatal heart attacks and strokes.

Thanks to your June '92 grant of $50,000, our team was able to complete research that enabled us to provide gene therapy to three patients. The results bode well for more widespread treatment. In fact, with your grant of $500,000, the St. George Institute of Molecular Research could extend its treatment capabilities to the international community.

The accompanying application details the research, procedures, and follow-up activities that we have implemented. Two independent analyses of our plans for facilities expansion, as well as the projected increase in treatment capability, are included. The enclosed vitae list the backgrounds and past experience of my clinical team.

Your consideration is greatly appreciated.

Sincerely,

Claudia A. Jackson

Claudia A. Jackson, Ph.D.

28. It's Never Too Late _____

15 errors—2 content; 3 grammar; 7 punctuation;
3 usage

It's Never Too Late Errors

Do you ever think, "If I was[1] more
energetic, I'd start exercising?[2]" Although
people often feel this way, it's never too
late to start exercising. Seniors who start
exercise programs are surprised to find
that their energy [3]level increases[3],[4] and
that heart and expiration[5] rates improve.
Increased weight loss is also a benefit;
brisk walking for 30[6] minutes can burn
350 calories. In some instances, existing
health problems such as adult[7] onset
diabetes has[8] improved after the implementation of an exercise program. According to a long-term study of Harvard
graduates, middle-aged and older men,[9]
who take up moderately vigorous exercise,[9] have up to a 41% reduction in coronary artery disease. Another study indicates that this[10] may keep arteries more
flexible, lessening the degree of arterial
hardening in older athletes.

Scientists have discovered that weight-
bearing exercise can help to decrease the
effects of osteoporosis, a loss of bone mass
especially common in older women. The
*Journal of the American Medical Associa-
tion* reported the results of an eight-week
weight-training program for a group of 86
to 96 year old's[11],[12] the group improved
its[13] muscle strength, which enabled them
to become more mobile and self-sufficient.

Scientists have conclude[14] that many of
what we consider the "normal symptoms
of aging" may be[15] in part[15] symptoms of
inactivity. The progressive dysfunction
associated with aging may be postponed
somewhat by regular aerobic exercise.

Scientists expect that further benefits of
exercise will be revealed as research
continues.

1. "If I *were*—Grammar: subjunctive
   mood used in contrary-to-fact statement **[3.32]**
2. *exercising*"?—Punctuation: question
   mark used outside quotation marks
   when it doesn't apply to quoted material **[5.59]**
3. their energy *levels increase*—Usage:
   agreement of noun and verb with
   possessive pronoun in number **[4.1]**
4. *increase* and—Punctuation: unnecessary comma **[5.41 j]**
5. *respiration* rates—Content: see caption **[2.1]**
6. *60* minutes—Content: see chart **[2.1]**
   (Acceptable: for *an hour* can)
7. *adult-onset* diabetes—Punctuation:
   hyphen used in compound adjective
   [5.48]
8. *have* improved—Usage: agreement of
   verb with subject (health problems/
   have) **[4.3]**
9. *men who...exercise have*—Punctuation:
   commas unnecessary with essential
   clause **[5.41 i]**
10. that *exercise* may—Grammar: general
    pronoun reference **[3.19]**
11. 96 year *olds*—Punctuation: apostro-
    phe unnecessary **[5.3]**
12. *olds. The*—Punctuation: use period to
    correct comma splice **[5.52]**
    (Acceptable: *olds:* the)
13. group improved *their*—Usage: agree-
    ment of possessive pronoun with
    collective subject used in plural sense
    [4.5]
14. have *concluded*—Grammar: past
    participle (used in present perfect
    tense) **[3.27, 3.29]**
15. may be, in *part*, symptoms—Punctua-
    tion: commas used with sentence
    interrupter **[5.28]**

It's Never Too Late Corrected

Do you ever think, "If I were more

energetic, I'd start exercising"? Although people often feel this way, it's never too late to start exercising. Seniors who start exercise programs are surprised to find that their energy levels increase and that heart and respiration rates improve. Increased weight loss is also a benefit; brisk walking for 60 minutes can burn 350 calories. In some instances, existing health problems such as adult-onset diabetes have improved after the implementation of an exercise program. According to a long-term study of Harvard graduates, middle-aged and older men who take up moderately vigorous exercise have up to a 41% reduction in coronary artery disease. Another study indicates that exercise may keep arteries more flexible, lessening the degree of arterial hardening in older athletes.

Scientists have discovered that weight-bearing exercise can help to decrease the effects of osteoporosis, a loss of bone mass especially common in older women. The *Journal of the American Medical Association* reported the results of an eight-week weight-training program for a group of 86 to 96 year olds. The group improved their muscle strength, which enabled them to become more mobile and self-sufficient.

Scientists have concluded that many of what we consider the "normal symptoms of aging" may be, in part, symptoms of inactivity. The progressive dysfunction associated with aging may be postponed somewhat by regular aerobic exercise. Scientists expect that further benefits of exercise will be revealed as research continues.

29. Drawing on Psychology

16 errors—2 content; 2 grammar; 5 punctuation; 7 usage

Drawing on Psychology Errors

The question is[1] Which posts are farther away? In reality, we know that all of the "posts" are [2]from our eyes the same distance[2]. They are simply marks on a two-dimensional page. On the other hand, when drawn with the proper surroundings, the smaller posts will appear farther[3] away. Psychological affects[4] such as perceptual context allows[5] the artist to fool the observer into seeing two[6] dimensions. (Here, the artist has made the first post 120[7]% of the size of the second in order to create the illusion of distance).[8]

Psychology works both ways. Most of us let our knowledge of real size effect[9] our drawing,[10] the resulting pictures appear unrealistically[11]. The artist must constantly be vigilant in order to draw things as they appear[12] not as they are [13]known to really[13] be. Farther[14], an artist must maintain their[15] vigilance, as well as enthusiasm, through many trials and errors. You might say that artists really have to get "psyched[16]!

1. question *is*,—Punctuation: comma introduces question within sentence **[5.35]**
2. are *the same distance from our eyes.*—Usage: misplaced modifier **[4.15]**
3. *farther*—Usage: word pair (further/farther) **[4.18]**
4. *effects*—Usage: word pair (affect/effect) **[4.18]**
5. *allow*—Usage: agreement of subject with verb (effects/allow) **[4.3]**
6. *three*—Content: see caption (picture is in two dimensions); you can deduce from the story and illustration that artists use two-dimensional tricks to simulate three dimensions **[2.1]**
7. *150%*—Content: see illustration (the first post on the left is one and a half times the size of the second) **[2.1]**
8. distance.)—Punctuation: period inside parenthesis **[5.55]**
9. *affect*—Usage: word pair (effect/affect) **[4.18]**
10. *drawing;* the—Punctuation: semicolon separates main clauses joined without

coordinating conjunctions (corrects comma splice) **[5.68]**

11. *unrealistic*—Grammar: adjective modifies noun (unrealistic pictures) **[3.1]**

12. *appear,* not—Punctuation: commas with contrasting expressions **[5.34]** (Acceptable: appear *and* not)

13. *really known to* be—Grammar: don't split infinitive **[3.40]**

14. *Further*—Usage: word pair (further/farther) **[4.18]**

15. *his*—Usage: agreement of possessive pronoun with noun in number **[4.2]**

16. *"psyched"*!—Punctuation: quotation marks denote special word usage (exclamation point goes outside quotation marks) **[5.64, 5.45]**

Drawing on Psychology Corrected

The question is, Which posts are farther away? In reality, we know that all of the "posts" are the same distance from our eyes. They are simply marks on a two-dimensional page. On the other hand, when drawn with the proper surroundings, the smaller posts will appear farther away. Psychological effects such as perceptual context allow the artist to fool the observer into seeing three dimensions. (Here, the artist has made the first post 150% of the size of the second in order to create the illusion of distance.)

Psychology works both ways. Most of us let our knowledge of real size affect our drawing; the resulting pictures appear unrealistic. The artist must constantly be vigilant in order to draw things as they appear, not as they are really known to be. Further, an artist must maintain his vigilance, as well as enthusiasm, through many trials and errors. You might say that artists really have to get "psyched"!

30. On Track

15 errors—2 content; 9 punctuation; 4 usage

On Track Errors

Gaining speed as they traveled south[1] past Hockett Station was[2] the old engine #678 and its five attached cars. They were going so fast that they seemed to be flying down the track. On the intersecting road,[3] traveled a family station wagon. It was now 9:15 A.M., and the signal light at the intersection was stuck on red[4]. A crash seemed eminent[5]! Rosie, the train's engineer, simply frowned, reached down, and plucked the car off the road.

"When will I ever get that signal to work right,[6]" she asked herself as her model steam engine raced harmlessly past. "It's anyones[7] guess as to when I'll get the time. Right now I have other things to deal with."

She took the broken,[8] red caboose from the track where it laid[9] and placed it on a track,[10] where it was out of the way. Various other tasks awaited her attention[11] rebuilding a failing engine, creating new landscape pieces, and laying track for a new route. For Rosie and her brothers, Nick and Theodore, these kind[12] of tasks were a labor of love.

Of the three siblings, Nick was first to begin the model railroad hobby; after her brother,[13] Theodore,[13] became enthusiastic, Rosie picked it up. "It's not a childrens'[14] game, and it is a lot of work," say the three, [15]but we would never give up the railroading life![15]

1. *north*—Content: see illustration and caption (if morning sun is behind Hockett Station, then the train is headed north) **[2.1]**

2. *were*—Usage: agreement of verb with two subjects joined by *and* (engine #678 and its five attached cars/were) **[4.6]**

3. *road* traveled—Punctuation: comma unnecessary when introductory dependent phrase immediately precedes verb **[5.41 d]**

4. *green*—Content: see caption **[2.1]**
5. *imminent*—Usage: word pair (eminent/imminent) **[4.18]**
6. *right?"*—Punctuation: quoted question **[5.56]**
7. *anyone's*—Punctuation: 's used with possessive indefinite pronoun **[5.7]**
8. *broken* red caboose—Punctuation: comma unnecessary with noncoordinate adjectives **[5.41 c]**
9. *lay*—Usage: word pair (lay/lie) Note: *lay* is past tense of the verb *to lie* **[4.18]**
10. *track* where—Punctuation: comma unnecessary in essential clause **[5.41 i]**
11. *attention:*—Punctuation: colon introduces list of items **[5.10]**
12. these *kinds* of tasks—Usage: agreement of adjective with noun **[4.10]**
13. *brother Theodore* became—Punctuation: unnecessary commas (since Rosie has two brothers, we know that *Theodore* is an essential appositive) **[5.41 i]**
14. *children's*—Punctuation: 's with possessive of plural not ending in *s* **[5.6]**
15. *"but* we would never give up the railroading *life!"*—Punctuation: quotation marks enclose both parts of divided quotation (also, quoted exclamation) **[5.60, 5.44]**

On Track Corrected

Gaining speed as they traveled north past Hockett Station were the old engine #678 and its five attached cars. They were going so fast that they seemed to be flying down the track. On the intersecting road traveled a family station wagon. It was now 9:15 A.M., and the signal light at the intersection was stuck on green. A crash seemed imminent! Rosie, the train's engineer, simply frowned, reached down, and plucked the car off the road.

"When will I ever get that signal to work right?" she asked herself as her model steam engine raced harmlessly

past. "It's anyone's guess as to when I'll get the time. Right now I have other things to deal with."

She took the broken red caboose from the track where it lay and placed it on a track where it was out of the way. Various other tasks awaited her attention: rebuilding a failing engine, creating new landscape pieces, and laying track for a new route. For Rosie and her brothers, Nick and Theodore, these kinds of tasks were a labor of love.

Of the three siblings, Nick was first to begin the model railroad hobby; after her brother Theodore became enthusiastic, Rosie picked it up. "It's not a children's game, and it is a lot of work," say the three, "but we would never give up the railroading life!"

31. Scheduled for Success

15 errors—1 content; 4 grammar; 6 punctuation; 4 usage

Scheduled for Success Errors

Moira is aware that, in today's competitive world, the straight-A student or top-ranked athlete are[1] no longer assured of acceptance at a top university (such as an Ivy League school;)[2] admissions officers are looking for qualified[3] well-rounded applicants. Moira is a[4] honor roll student taking seven college preparatory classes this semester and participating on the school debate team. She would also like to try out for the soccer team, which practices Tuesday and Thursday, but she already has a flute lesson on Tuesday. In order to add more activities to her busy schedule and leave some free time for her[5], Moira will have to manage her time efficiently.

First[6] Moira lists her activities for Tuesday. Then she tries to determine how to schedule them all. Tryouts for the soccer team is[7] at 4:00. Moira's flute lesson is at 5:30, but it is across town, and she will have to take the bus to get there. Moira is also working on a group history project, and everyone is expected to bring their[8] part of the project to a meeting Tuesday night at 6:30. The group is meeting at a classmate's house near Moira's flute teachers[9, 10] so she can walk or take the bus to her meeting.

If Moira leaves the soccer tryouts at 5:00, she can like[11] take the 5:10 bus from school to the corner of Oak and Elm, arriving at 5:25, and then walk to her teacher's house on Oak Street. If she is late leaving the tryouts, she can take the next bus, which leaves school at 5:20. This[12] will drop her at Oak and Elm at 5:25[13]. Her classmate's house is six blocks away on Maple. If Moira finishes her flute lesson by 6:00, she can walk to the meeting,[14] if her flute lesson runs late, she will [15]have caught[15] the 6:15 bus at the corner of Oak and Elm and the bus will drop her at Maple and Elm by 6:20.

1. athlete *is*—Usage: agreement of verb with closer of two subjects joined by *or* **[4.6]**
2. *school);*—Punctuation: semicolon outside parenthesis **[5.71]**
3. *qualified,* well-rounded—Punctuation: comma used with coordinate adjectives **[5.24]**
4. *an* honor—Grammar: article *an* before vowel sound **[3.5]**
5. for *herself*—Grammar: reflexive pronoun **[3.25]**
6. *First,*—Punctuation: comma used after introductory word **[5.25]**
7. *are*—Usage: agreement of verb with subject (tryouts/are) **[4.3]**
8. *his* part—Usage: agreement of possessive pronoun with indefinite pronoun (everyone/his) **[4.9]**
   (Acceptable: *her* part or *his/her* part)
9. *teacher's*—Punctuation: *'s* used with singular possessive **[5.4]**
   (Acceptable: *teacher's house*)
10. *teacher's,* so—Punctuation: comma

used before coordinating conjunction (from the caption, we can infer that the purpose for meeting at the classmate's house is not linked to Moira's being able to walk from her teacher's house) **[5.37]**
11. *can take*—Usage: unnecessary word **[4.19]**
12. *This bus* will drop—Grammar: general pronoun reference **[3.19]**
13. *5:35*—Content: see illustration **[2.1]**
14. *meeting;* if—Punctuation: semicolon separates main clauses joined without coordinating conjunction (corrects comma splice) **[5.68]**
15. will *catch*—Grammar: future tense (error is based on timing of events in context: if Moira is late leaving her flute lesson, she could not have already caught the 6:15 bus) **[3.29]**

Scheduled for Success Corrected

Moira is aware that, in today's competitive world, the straight-A student or top-ranked athlete is no longer assured of acceptance at a top university (such as an Ivy League school); admissions officers are looking for qualified, well-rounded applicants. Moira is an honor roll student taking seven college preparatory classes this semester and participating on the school debate team. She would also like to try out for the soccer team, which practices Tuesday and Thursday, but she already has a flute lesson on Tuesday. In order to add more activities to her busy schedule and leave some free time for herself, Moira will have to manage her time efficiently.

First, Moira lists her activities for Tuesday. Then she tries to determine how to schedule them all. Tryouts for the soccer team are at 4:00. Moira's flute lesson is at 5:30, but it is across town, and she will have to take the bus to get there. Moira is also working on a group history project, and everyone is expected to bring his part of the project to a meeting Tuesday night at 6:30. The group is meeting at a classmate's house near Moira's flute teacher's, so she can walk or take the bus to her meeting.

If Moira leaves the soccer tryouts at 5:00, she can take the 5:10 bus from school to the corner of Oak and Elm, arriving at 5:25, and then walk to her teacher's house on Oak Street. If she is late leaving the tryouts, she can take the next bus, which leaves school at 5:20. The bus will drop her at Oak and Elm at 5:35. Her classmate's house is six blocks away on Maple. If Moira finishes her flute lesson by 6:00, she can walk to the meeting; if her flute lesson runs late, she will catch the 6:15 bus at the corner of Oak and Elm and the bus will drop her at Maple and Elm by 6:20.

32. An Honest Fake

17 errors—3 content; 3 capitalization; 5 grammar; 5 punctuation; 1 usage

An Honest Fake Errors

Nothing but darkness meets his gaze. Only the fresh breath of spring[1] fills Les Anyman's nostrils as he staggers stiffly to his feet and works his wrists free from their bonds. He takes off his mask. He is all by him[2] in the woods. Next to him on the damp stones lie[3] an envelope. He reads the following:

If you want to be one
Of the guys whom[4] have fun
Then you must walk the earth
To show ourselves[5] your worth
Bring back the stuff
To prove you have enough
Of what it will take
To be an Honest Fake

"This is someones[6] idea of a test," Les thinks, racking his brain. Get[7] into the Honest Fakes is an honor, but you have to have animal magnetism and charm. You have to be able to carry a tune. You have to have good looks. In fact, you must be a

capital fellow all around. Les wonders if he can measure up?[8] Suddenly, he knows what to do!

From the park, Les heads east[9] to the Five and Dime and finds a small refrigerator magnet in the shape of a cow. [10]The next stop is the bookstore, where he buys a comic book and some note paper. (He also gets a list of cities including Albany, N.Y.,[11] San Francisco[12], California[13] and Jackson, Mississippi[14]). He then drops by the jeweler's to pick up a charm bracelet.[10] At the scenic point, he takes several "good looks" at the surrounding area and sketches them onto the note paper. He is now ready to head Northwest[15] to get the return bus to the clubhouse. He can hardly wait to knock on the clubhouse door. "It is me[16]," he will say, "[17]The newest member of the Honest Fakes."

1. *Spring*—Capital: season personified **[1.12]**
2. *himself*—Grammar: reflexive pronoun **[3.25]**
3. *lies*—Usage: agreement of verb with subject (envelope/lies) **[4.3]**
4. *who*—Grammar: pronoun *who* as subject of adjective clause **[3.26]**
5. *us*—Grammar: pronoun used as object (not reflexive) **[3.22]**
6. *someone's*—Punctuation: 's in possessive indefinite pronoun **[5.7]**
7. *Getting*—Grammar: verbal (gerund) **[3.38]**
8. *up.*—Punctuation: question mark unnecessary after indirect question **[5.57]**
9. *north*—Content: see map **[2.1]** Acceptable: *northwest*
10. *He then drops by...bracelet. The next stop*—Content: see map for correct sequence of events (move "jeweler" sentence so it precedes "bookstore" sentence) **[2.1]**
11. *N.Y.;*—Punctuation: semicolon separates items (in a series) containing commas **[5.70]**

12. Sacramento—Content: see caption ("list of state capitals"—capital of California is Sacramento) [2.1]
13. *California;*—Punctuation: semicolon separates items (in a series) containing commas [5.70]
14. *Mississippi.)*—Punctuation: period inside parenthesis [5.55]
15. *northwest*—Capital: unnecessary [1.6] (Acceptable: *north*)
16. "It is *I,*—Grammar: nominative case used with the verb "to be" [3.23]
17. say, *"the*—Capital: unnecessary (divided quotation) [1.2]

An Honest Fake Corrected

Nothing but darkness meets his gaze. Only the fresh breath of Spring fills Les Anyman's nostrils as he staggers stiffly to his feet and works his wrists free from their bonds. He takes off his mask. He is all by himself in the woods. Next to him on the damp stones lies an envelope. He reads the following:

If you want to be one
Of the guys who have fun
Then you must walk the earth
To show us your worth
Bring back the stuff
To prove you have enough
Of what it will take
To be an Honest Fake

"This is someone's idea of a test," Les thinks, racking his brain. Getting into the Honest Fakes is an honor, but you have to have animal magnetism and charm. You have to be able to carry a tune. You have to have good looks. In fact, you must be a capital fellow all around. Les wonders if he can measure up. Suddenly, he knows what to do!

From the park, Les heads north to the Five and Dime and finds a small refrigerator magnet in the shape of a cow. He then drops by the jeweler's to pick up a charm bracelet. The next stop is the bookstore, where he buys a comic book and some note paper. (He also gets a list of cities including Albany, N.Y.; Sacramento, California; and Jackson, Mississippi.) At the scenic point, he takes several "good looks" at the surrounding area and sketches them onto the note paper. He is now ready to head northwest to get the return bus to the clubhouse. He can hardly wait to knock on the clubhouse door. "It is I," he will say, "the newest member of the Honest Fakes."

33. Moore Money

16 errors—3 content; 1 capitalization; 1 grammar; 8 punctuation; 2 spelling; 1 usage

Moore Money Errors

Carlos Moore, Assistant Manager[1] at a fast-food restaurant, makes $5.00 an hour and works 15 hours a week. He also gets $15.00 a week doing the yard work, laundry[2] etc. at home. Currently, Carlos takes the bus to,[3] and from work. He has decided to buy his own "wheels;"[4] as a result[5] he needs to budget carefully to cover the additional expenses.

Carlos is given free meals at work[6] so he can cut down his food expenses; however[7] he still likes to eat out two or three times a week. On weekends, he goes to the movies ($7.00) or bowls two games ($2.50 shoes, $2.50/game.)[8] Sometimes he goes to the school basketball game ($5.00). He usually spends extra money on snacks.[9] When he's out. Each week, he allows $10.00 for school supplies such as stationary[10] and $10.00 for miscellaneous personal expenses. He puts $20.00 weekly in to[11] a college savings plan. He plans to split the cost of the car with his parents; he will be responsible for half the car payment ($68.00[12] weekly) and half the insurance ($6.25 weekly), plus gas.

Having list[13] all the prospective costs,[14] planning a budget is next. The pie charts show Carlos's current weekly expenses and his proposed expenses if he gets a car. In order to meet his additional costs, Carlos will have to eliminate about

$50.00[15] from his current weekly expenses. He does not want to touch the money for his college savings fund. He can easily eliminate the meals out and cut his entertainment costs by a third[16]. Carlos feels that it's worth "tightening his belt" if he can "broaden his horizons."

1. Moore, *assistant manager*—Capital: unnecessary (title not used as part of name) **[1.8]**
2. *laundry,* etc.—Punctuation: comma used after words in a series **[5.22]**
3. *to* and from—Punctuation: unnecessary comma **[5.41 j]**
4. *"wheels";*—Punctuation: semicolon falls outside quotation marks **[5.72]**
5. as a *result,*—Punctuation: comma used after introductory phrase **[5.26]**
6. *work,* so—Punctuation: comma used to avoid ambiguity (Note: *so* is also being used as a coordinating conjunction here) **[5.36]**
7. *however,* he—Punctuation: comma used after conjunctive adverb **[5.38]**
8. *game).*—Punctuation: period outside parenthesis **[5.55]**
9. *snacks when*—Punctuation: sentence fragment **[5.82]**
10. *stationery*—Spelling **[6.1]**
11. *into*—Spelling **[6.6]**
12. *($34.00* weekly)—Content: see caption and illustration (Note: $136 is half the monthly payment; this is then divided by 4 to determine average weekly payments.) **[2.1]**
13. Having *listed*—Grammar: verbal (participle) **[3.37]**
14. costs, *Carlos must plan a budget next.*—Usage: dangling modifier **[4.16]**
15. *$30*—Content: see caption and illustration (Note: In his current budget, Carlos has $12.50 in unallocated money. He can also deduct the $7.50 for bus fare from his proposed transportation costs. Since these can be

subtracted from the $49.25 needed for transportation, he only needs to eliminate $29.25.) **[2.1]**
16. by *half*—Content: see illustration **[2.1]**

Moore Money Corrected

Carlos Moore, assistant manager at a fast-food restaurant, makes $5.00 an hour and works 15 hours a week. He also gets $15.00 a week doing yard work, laundry, etc. at home. Currently, Carlos takes the bus to and from work. He has decided to buy his own "wheels"; as a result, he needs to budget carefully to cover the additional expenses.

Carlos is given free meals at work, so he can cut down his food expenses; however, he still likes to eat out two or three times a week. On weekends, he goes to the movies ($7.00) or bowls two games ($2.50 shoes, $2.50/game). Sometimes he goes to the school basketball game ($5.00). He usually spends extra money on snacks when he's out. Each week, he allows $10.00 for school supplies such as stationery and $10.00 for miscellaneous personal expenses. He puts $20.00 weekly into a college savings plan. He plans to split the cost of the car with his parents; he will be responsible for half the car payment ($34.00 weekly) and half the insurance ($6.25 weekly), plus gas.

Having listed all the prospective costs, Carlos must plan a budget next. The pie charts show Carlos's current weekly expenses and his proposed expenses if he gets a car. In order to meet his additional costs, Carlos will have to eliminate about $30 from his current weekly expenses. He does not want to touch the money for his college savings fund. He can easily eliminate the meals out and cut his entertainment costs by half. Carlos feels that it's worth "tightening his belt" if he can "broaden his horizons."

GUIDE TO GRAMMAR, USAGE, AND PUNCTUATION

The punctuation, grammar, and usage guidelines that follow cover all the skills used in this book. These skills represent an advanced-level English curriculum. This guide is not meant to be a complete English reference but rather an aid in improving written and spoken English.

The types of errors are broken down into these areas: capitalization, content, grammar, usage, punctuation, and spelling.

CAPITALIZATION

1.1 Capitalize the first word in a sentence.
>What a day we had!

1.2 Capitalize the first word in a direct quote. Do not capitalize the first word in the second half of a divided quotation or the first word of a sentence fragment.
>Jose said, "Come and look at the beautiful new mural on display in the library."
>"Come," Jose said, "and look at the beautiful new mural on display in the library."
>Jose said that he wanted us to see "the beautiful new mural."

1.3 Capitalize the first word of a statement or question within a sentence.
>The question is, Will he be able to complete the project?
>Always remember, What goes up must come down.

1.4 Use a capital letter for a proper noun. A proper noun names a specific person, place, or thing. (In general, a noun that is not proper should be lower case.)
>Paris, France   the World Series   John Doe

1.5 Use a capital letter for a proper adjective. A proper adjective is derived from a proper noun. (In general, an adjective that is not proper should be lower case.)
>French cooking   African tribes   a Southern accent

1.6 Do not capitalize compass directions unless they refer to a specific recognized region. (A clue is that specific regions are often preceded by *the*.)
>We are going south this summer.   We are going to the South this summer.
>We are headed west.   We are visiting the West Coast.

1.7 Use a capital letter on the abbreviated form of proper nouns and proper adjectives.
>Nov. 27   U.C.L.A.

1.8 Use a capital letter on titles and their abbreviated forms when they are used as part of a name or in place of a name. However, do not capitalize titles when they are not used as part of a name or in place of a name.

Captain John Smith   John Smith was the captain.

Yes, Captain, the lieutenant left at noon.

Dr. Susan White   We saw the doctor.

Oh, Doctor, how much of this medicine do I take?

Astronomer Lowel   Mr. Lowel, noted astronomer.

We spoke with noted astronomer Percival Lowel.

Usage note: Beware of a tendency to overcapitalize. Many people want to capitalize titles regardless of their position. As a rule of thumb, if you can replace the title with the person's name (or if the title precedes the name and is used as part of it), then it is appropriate to capitalize the title.

1.9 Capitalize academic degrees when they follow a name.

Susan White, M.D.   James Herriott, D.V.M.   Rita MacIntyre, Ph.D.

1.10 Capitalize words of familial relation only when used in place of a name.

At 1:00, Mother called us in for lunch.

My mother called us in for lunch.

1.11 Capitalize the days of the week, the months, and the holidays.

Monday, December 24   New Year's Day

1.12 Capitalize a season only when it is being personified.

autumn leaves   summer vacation   as Winter grasped us in its chilly hands

1.13 Do not capitalize school subjects (except for proper nouns or adjectives) unless they are followed by a course number.

American history   chemistry   algebra

French   British Literature II   Algebra 2A

1.14 Always capitalize the first and last words in titles of books, stories, articles, movies, paintings, and other works of art. Capitalize all other words except for articles (*a, an, the*), coordinating conjunctions (*and, but, or, nor*), prepositions of five letters or fewer (*in, with, on,* etc.), and the *to* in infinitives.

For Whom the Bell Tolls   *In the Heat of the Night*   *Gone with the Wind*

Noodlehead Stories from Around the World   *Hansel and Gretel*

"Love Is a Many Splendored Thing"   *How to Succeed in Business*

Usage note: Style manuals disagree about capitalizing prepositions in titles. More conservative manuals say that prepositions should not be capitalized regardless of length (unless they are the first or last word in the title). The trend, however, seems to be toward capitalizing the longer prepositions (*through, around,* etc.) and leaving shorter prepositions lower case. The cutoff in length seems to be around five letters, and you will see prepositions like *under* styled both upper case and lower case.

CONTENT 2.1 In *Editor in Chief*®, content errors occur only where the story contradicts the caption or illustration, which are correct. Some content errors will be simple differences in information between an illustration/caption and the story. Other content errors will require the student to analyze information from the illustration/caption in order to correct the paragraph.

Note: There has been a trend toward dropping the negative in the expression "couldn't care less" ("could care less"); the resulting expression means the opposite of what is usually intended. (If I *could* care less, then I must already care.)

GRAMMAR   Parts of Speech

Adjectives and Adverbs

Both adjectives and adverbs modify (give information about) other words and, hence, are referred to by the general term "modifiers."

Adjectives

3.1 Adjectives tell what kind (*small* house), which one (*new* hat), or how many (*one* child). Adjectives modify nouns or pronouns. See "Problems with Modifiers," p. 107, for more information.

3.2 The demonstrative adjectives *this* and *these* are used to indicate something that is nearby, while *that* and *those* are used to indicate something that is farther away.

Nearby: *this* house, *these* houses

Farther away: *that* house, *those* houses

3.3 Here and there are unnecessary with *this, that, these,* and *those.*

Incorrect: this here box

Correct: this box

See "Comparing and Contrasting Adjectives and Adverbs," p. 79, for more information on using adjectives. See "Demonstrative Pronouns," p. 87, for more on *this, that, these,* and *those.* See "Participle as Verbal," p. 97, for information on participles as adjectives.

Adverbs

3.4 Adverbs modify verbs, adjectives, or other adverbs. Adverbs tell how, when, where, how often, how much, or to what extent. Regular adverbs are formed by adding *-ly* to an adjective; however, not all words that end in *-ly* are adverbs, and not all adverbs end in *-ly.*

Example: She ran *quickly.* (*quickly* modifies verb—tells how she ran)

Example: I swam *yesterday.* (*yesterday* modifies verb—tells when I swam)

Example: He walked *downtown.* (downtown modifies verb—tells where he walked)

Example: It is *very rarely* hot here. (very modifies adverb; rarely modifies adjective—together they tell how often it is hot)

Example: That is an *extremely* beautiful apple. (extremely modifies adjective—tells to what extent the apple is beautiful)

See "Comparing and Contrasting Adjectives and Adverbs," p. 79, for more on using adverbs.

Articles

3.5   Articles (a, an, the) are adjectives. Use *an* before a vowel sound, *a* before a consonant sound. Confusion over which article to use most often comes with words beginning in *h*. If the word clearly begins with a vowel or consonant sound, the standard rule for articles applies. Confusion usually comes in words beginning with *h* in which the *h* is part of an unstressed or lightly stressed first syllable. In such cases, it is considered acceptable to use either *a* or *an*.

Examples: an hour, a ham

Examples: a historian or an historian, a heroic or an heroic

Comparative and Superlative Forms of Adjectives and Adverbs

3.6   Comparative and superlative forms of adjectives and adverbs are used to compare the degrees of characteristics possessed by the objects that they modify.

Most one-syllable adjectives/adverbs add the suffix *-er* or *-est*.

hot—hotter—hottest   small—smaller—smallest
lucky—luckier—luckiest

Some adjectives/adverbs use more/most to create the comparative and superlative forms.

quietly—more quietly—most quietly
beautiful—more beautiful—most beautiful
difficult—more difficult—most difficult

Less and *least* can also be used to create comparative and superlative forms. (Note that in some modifiers, the base word is unaltered.)

aggressive—less aggressive—least aggressive
powerful—less powerful—least powerful

Irregular comparative forms

good/well—better—best

bad—worse—worst

many/much—more—most

Whether you use the comparative or superlative form depends on how many things are being compared.

Comparative: The comparative form of adjectives and adverbs is used when comparing two things.

He is the *older* of two children. (adjective)

The Jets are *better* than the Eagles. (adjective)

She runs *faster* than the boys. (adverb) *Note that she is not part of the boys.*

Superlative: The superlative form is used when comparing more than two things.

> He is the *oldest* child of seven. (adjective)
>
> The Jets are the *sharpest* of all the teams. (adjective)
>
> She is the *best* player on the team. (adjective) *Note that she is part of the team.*
>
> He sings the *most beautifully*. (adverb)

Comparing and Contrasting Adjectives and Adverbs

3.7   Most (but not all) adverbs end in *-ly*. Adjectives usually don't end in *-ly* (although a few do). Sometimes the same word functions as an adjective and an adverb. Sometimes adverbs of a particular word have more than one form. See the examples below.

Adjective	Adverb	Adverb ending in *-ly*
a *high* window	He leaped *high*.	We think *highly* of him.
a *close* encounter	He walked *close* to her.	We watched her *closely*.

Adjective ending in *-ly*	Adverb
nightly train	We go *nightly*.
lively tune	Step *lively*, boys!

These examples show that distinguishing between adverbs and adjectives is not as simple as checking to see whether a word ends in *-ly*. You need to see what the word modifies (describes).

Adjectives modify	Adverbs modify
nouns	verbs
pronouns	adjectives
	other adverbs

> Adjective: It rained *last* night. (*last* tells which night; it modifies the noun *night*)
>
> Adverb: Our team played *last*. (*last* tells when the team played; it modifies the verb *played*)

Linking verbs are frequently followed by adjectives.

> Adjective: She looked *pretty*. (*pretty* modifies the subject she)
>
> Adjective: He sounded *happy*. (*happy* modifies the subject he)
>
> Adjective: He felt *bad*. (*bad* modifies the subject he)

Many verbs that function as linking verbs can also be used as action verbs. In these cases, the action verbs will be followed by adverbs rather than adjectives.

> Linking verb with adjective: He stayed *quiet*. (*quiet* modifies the subject he)
>
> Action verb with adverb: He stayed *quietly* in his seat. (*quietly* modifies the verb stayed; it tells how he stayed in his seat)

Linking verbs take adjectives. Action verbs take adverbs. See "Linking Verbs," p. 96.

Coordinate and Noncoordinate Modifiers

3.8   Two or more adjectives or adverbs can combine to modify a word or phrase. The exact relationship between the modifiers and the word they modify is conveyed by punctuation: coordinate modifiers are separated by commas, noncoordinate modifiers do not take any punctuation.

3.9 **Coordinate modifiers:** Coordinate modifiers are two (or more) adjectives or adverbs that equally and separately modify a word or phrase. To determine if the modifiers are coordinate, insert *and* between the modifiers and listen to how the sentence sounds or reverse the order of the modifiers and see if the meaning remains the same. If the sentence still works with these changes, then the modifiers are coordinate modifiers.

> Coordinate adjectives: She was a loyal, conscientious person.
>
> Test: She was a loyal *and* conscientious person. She was a conscientious, loyal person.
>
> Coordinate adverbs: The seal swam smoothly, gracefully through the water.
>
> Test: The seal swam smoothly *and* gracefully through the water. The seal swam gracefully, smoothly through the water.

Coordinate modifiers are separated by commas.

3.10 **Noncoordinate adjectives:** Adjectives are noncoordinate when one adjective modifies the noun plus the adjective that immediately precedes the noun; for example, in the phrase "the first spring flower," *first* and *spring* do not modify flower in the same way. *First* modifies the noun (flower) plus the adjective that immediately precedes it (spring); that is, *first* modifies the combined phrase, "spring flower." We are not describing the first flower or the first spring, but the first flower of spring. Some examples of noncoordinate adjectives are listed below.

> big orange cat (*big* modifies orange cat)
>
> chewy oatmeal cookies (*chewy* modifies oatmeal cookies)
>
> excellent football player (*excellent* modifies football player)

You can use the test for coordinate modifiers to help recognize noncoordinate modifiers. If you make the test changes and the sentence no longer has the same meaning, then the modifiers are noncoordinate.

> Test "big orange cat": big *and* orange cat; orange big cat
>
> Test "chewy oatmeal cookies": chewy *and* oatmeal cookies; oatmeal chewy cookies
>
> Test "excellent football player": excellent *and* football player; football excellent player

The tests show that the first adjective is modifying the noun plus the adjective immediately preceding the noun.

There should be no punctuation between noncoordinate adjectives.

Compound Adjectives

3.11 Compound adjectives are unit modifiers, words that work together as a unit to modify a noun or pronoun; for example, when we say "a quick-thinking speaker" we do not mean a quick speaker or a thinking speaker, but a speaker who thinks quickly. Although compound adjectives function as adjectives, they may be composed of not only adjectives but also adverbs, nouns, participles, and even verbs. Some examples of compound adjectives are listed below.

high-risk ventures	more-organized approach	fleece-lined coat
all-out effort	well-documented complaint	much-loved pet
blue-green algae	better-known candidate	50-yard dash

Phrases may also function as compound adjectives.

a spur-of-the-moment decision   how-to books   a face-the-facts meeting

To prevent confusion and to ease reading, compound adjectives are generally hyphenated when they immediately precede the noun that they modify. The example below demonstrates how meaning can differ with and without the hyphen.

He will be satisfied only with some more intricate plans. (He already has some intricate plans but wants more of them.)

He will be satisfied only with some more-intricate plans. (He has some plans but wants some that are more intricate.)

Compound adjectives that are so well known that misreading is unlikely are rarely hyphenated.

high school classes	sodium chloride solution	blood pressure cuff
Civil War stories	per capita income	dry goods store

Note that when an adverb ending in -*ly* modifies an adjective that is modifying a noun, no punctuation falls between the adverb and the adjective, as adverb + adjective + noun is the normal word order.

a highly disputed case   an overly anxious manner   the widely held opinion

In some cases, compound adjectives are also hyphenated when acting as a predicate adjective (following a linking verb) if they still function as a unit modifier.

That dog is good-looking.   He seems tough-minded.

See also "Coordinate and Noncoordinate Modifiers," p. 79, for more information.

Participles Used as Adjectives

3.12   The present or past participle forms of verbs can be used as adjectives to modify nouns or pronouns. In the examples below, the same participle is shown used as an adjective and as a part of the verb. (In the latter case, the verb phrase is *be* + participle.)

Adjective—present participle: The *crying* child ran to his mother. (*crying* modifies child)

Verb phrase—present participle: The child was *crying* as he ran to his mother. (*was crying* is the verb phrase)

Adjective—past participle: The *tired* child ran to his mother. (*tired* modifies child)

Verb phrase—past participle: The child had *tired* himself by running to his mother. (*had tired* is the verb phrase)

See "Participles as Verbs," p. 96, for more on participles as verbs.

Well/Good

3.13   As modifiers, *well* and *good* are sometimes a source of confusion. *Well* is both an adverb and an adjective while *good* is only an adjective. Perhaps some of the confusion comes because *well* and *good* occasionally overlap in meaning. You can say either "He feels well" or "He feels good" to indicate a general state of health. *Good* is not just limited to describing health, however. You can say "He feels good about his promotion." *Well* cannot be used in this way. As an adjective, *well* has only three meanings:

1. to be healthy
   He looks *well*.
2. to look well-dressed or well-groomed
   He looks *well* in a suit.
3. to be satisfactory, right, or proper
   It is *well* to fulfill your commitments.

Good, on the other hand, is always an adjective. It cannot be used to modify a verb. In the examples below, *well* and *good* convey similar meanings, but they do so by modifying different types of words.

Good: You did a *good* job. (*good* is an adjective; it modifies job)

Well: You did *well*. (*well* is an adverb; it modifies did)

Another source of confusion may be that the comparative and superlative forms are the same for *good* and *well*: good, better, best and well, better, best. See "Comparative and Superlative Forms of Adjectives and Adverbs," p. 78.

Conjunctions

The word *conjunction* refers to joining or coming together. We use conjunctions to join various grammatical elements: words, phrases, clauses. There are three kinds of conjunctions: coordinating, correlative, and subordinating. Each of these three types of conjunctions is described below.

Coordinating Conjunctions

3.14   Coordinating conjunctions join words, phrases, clauses, or sentences. The word *coordinating* indicates that the elements that are joined have equal grammatical weight—for example, nouns with other nouns, verbs with other verbs, clauses with other clauses of equal rank.

He *ran and jumped*. (verb with verb)

We could use a new *car or truck*. (noun with noun)

I saw *two of my friends but none of my relatives* at the wedding. (2 phrases)

She had a new computer, so she took a class on home computing. (2 independent clauses)

There are seven coordinating conjunctions. To assist in remembering these conjunctions, use their first letters to form a mnemonic aid:

FAN BOYS—**f**or, **a**nd, **n**or, **b**ut, **o**r, **y**et, **s**o. *And, but, or,* and *nor* are always used as coordinating conjunctions; *for, yet,* and *so* do not always function as coordinating conjunctions. In fact, *for* and *yet* are rarely used as conjunctions. Use the tricks below to decide whether *for, yet,* and *so* are functioning as conjunctions.

For usually functions as a preposition and is often found at the beginning of prepositional phrases. When *for* can be replaced by the word *because*, *for* is functioning as a conjunction.

> Preposition: We are going home *for* lunch.
>
> Conjunction: We are going home, *for* lunch is served at 1:00. (*for* means because)

Yet usually functions as an adverb referring to time. When *yet* can be replaced by *but* or *nevertheless*, it is functioning as a conjunction.

> Adverb: We are not *yet* ready to go.
>
> Conjunction: We are not ready, *yet* we will go. (*yet* means but)

So usually functions as an adverb that intensifies the word it modifies. *So* is also commonly used as shorthand for *so that* (a subordinating conjunction). When *so* can be replaced by *thus* or *therefore*, it is functioning as a coordinating conjunction.

> Adverb: That dog is *so* strong.
>
> Subordinating conjunction: We need a strong dog *so* he can pull our sled. (*so* is short for so that)
>
> Coordinating conjunction: That dog is strong, *so* we used him to pull our sled. (*so* means therefore)

Note that in the examples above, when *for, yet,* and *so* function as coordinating conjunctions, they are preceded by commas. When a coordinating conjunction joins two independent clauses, or main clauses, the conjunction should be preceded by a comma unless the independent clauses are short and closely related.

> We went to Paris, but we stayed only a few days.
>
> He came and he went.

See "Parallel Structure," p. 106, for more on using coordinating conjunctions.

Correlative Conjunctions

3.15   Correlative conjunctions is the name given to conjunctions used in pairs. The following are common correlative conjunctions:

> either...or   neither...nor   both...and   not only...but (also)
> whether...or

As with coordinating conjunctions, correlative conjunctions join elements of similar grammatical construction, e.g., two adjectives, two prepositional phrases, two independent clauses, etc. Another way to think of this is that correlative conjunctions join constructions that are parallel. Correlative conjunctions should be placed as close as possible to the elements they join.

Misplaced: Either *we will go to the lake* or *to the seashore.* (joins independent clause and prepositional phrase)

Correct: We will go either *to the lake* or *to the seashore.* (joins 2 prepositional phrases)

In general, correlative conjunctions do not require commas; however, they may need a comma if they join two independent clauses. In the first example below, *not only…but* joins two independent clauses. In the second example, the same correlative conjunction joins two nouns (*cat* and *dog*).

Not only do we have to wash the car, but we also must shampoo the carpets.

We have not only a cat but also a dog.

Subordinating Conjunctions

3.16   Subordinating conjunctions join subordinate, or dependent, clauses to independent clauses. The following are commonly used subordinating conjunctions:

after	before	since	when
although	even though	so that	whenever
as	how	than	where
as if	if	that	wherever
as though	in order that	though	whether
as much as	inasmuch as	unless	while
because	provided	until	

Anytime a subordinating conjunction begins a clause, that clause will be a subordinate clause. This is true even if the clause that follows the conjunction would otherwise be an independent clause.

Independent clause: we left the party

Subordinate (dependent) clause: after we left the party

Some of the subordinating conjunctions also function as other parts of speech: *after, as, before, once, since,* and *until* sometimes function as prepositions; *how, when,* and *where* can be adverbs; *that* is often a relative or demonstrative pronoun. To determine whether one of these words is functioning as a subordinating conjunction or some other part of speech, remember first that subordinating conjunctions join words or groups of words.

Adverb: *How* does he do it?

Subordinating conjunction: We don't know *how* he does it.

Relative pronoun: *That* dog was so large.

Subordinating conjunction: We did not know *that* the dog was so large.

It would be easy if a subordinating conjunction always had to be in the middle of the words it joins; however, subordinating conjunctions can begin sentences. Prepositions also frequently begin sentences. To distinguish between a preposition and a subordinating conjunction, look for the first noun or pronoun that follows the word in question. If that noun or pronoun is the subject of a clause, then the word in question is a subordinating conjunction. If the noun or pronoun is not the subject of a clause, the word is a preposition. In other words, the second clue to remember is that subordinating conjunctions always begin clauses, not phrases.

> Preposition: *Before* the meeting, we want to get coffee. (*meeting* is not the subject of a clause)

> Subordinating conjunction: *Before* the meeting begins, we want to get coffee. (*meeting* is the subject of a clause, "the meeting begins")

3.17   **Commas with dependent clauses:** In general, when a sentence consists of a dependent clause followed by an independent clause, the dependent clause should be followed by a comma.

> Dependent clause + independent clause: After we left the party, we went for a walk.

> Dependent clause + independent clause: While the neighbors were away, the dog dug up the roses.

In general, when a dependent clause follows an independent clause, no comma is required.

> Independent clause + dependent clause: We went for a walk after we left the party.

> Independent clause + dependent clause: The dog dug up the roses while the neighbors were away.

Beginning writers often insert commas before clauses beginning with the conjunctions *since* and *because*. *Since* and *because*, however, are subordinating, not coordinating, conjunctions. This means that even if *since* or *because* is followed by an independent clause, that clause is made subordinate by *since* or *because*. Such sentences containing *since* or *because* are examples of independent clauses + dependent clauses and do not require a comma.

> Example: We went right home from the store because we were afraid the ice cream would melt.

> Example: I wanted to ask him about the football game since I knew he had seen it.

For more on independent and dependent clauses, see "Clauses," p. 99, and "Clauses and Punctuation," p. 121.

3.18   **Essential and nonessential clauses:** Essential (restrictive) and nonessential (nonrestrictive) dependent clauses compose a special subcategory of dependent clauses. As their names imply, essential clauses are essential to the meaning of a sentence. Nonessential clauses are not essential to the meaning of a sentence. Nonessential clauses can be removed from a sentence without altering the basic meaning of the sentence.

As an example of the essential clause, consider the following: We want to point out a male friend who is standing with a number of other men, so we need to give some information that will help our audience to identify the specific man we are referring to. We mention that the man is wearing a red hat as an aid in identifying him. The sentence would read as shown below.

> Essential: The man who is wearing a red hat is a friend of mine.

As an example of the nonessential clause, consider the following: We want to point out the same male friend, but this time there are no other men near him. We mention that he is wearing a red hat, but we are not using that fact as a means to identify him; we just add the information about the hat for a bit of interest.

> Nonessential: That man, who is wearing a red hat, is a friend of mine.

In the examples above, the dependent clause "who is wearing a red hat" functions as an essential or a nonessential clause depending upon the meaning of the sentence. Commas are needed if the clause is nonessential; however, if the clause is essential to the meaning of the sentence, commas are not used. Consider the examples below.

> Nonessential: Jason, who always gets into trouble, broke the vase.
> Essential: The brother who always gets into trouble broke the vase.

In the first example above, we know that Jason broke the vase. The clause set off by commas gives us more information about Jason, but we do not need that information to identify him. In the second example, however, the clause "who always gets into trouble" tells us which brother it was who broke the vase; therefore, this clause is essential.

See "Clauses and Punctuation," p. 121, for more on essential and nonessential clauses.

Pronouns

A pronoun is used in place of a noun or nouns (antecedent) to which the pronoun refers.

Clear Reference

3.19 When using a pronoun, make certain that the antecedent of the pronoun is clear. Unless the reader knows to what noun or nouns a pronoun is referring, the sentence becomes meaningless or confusing. For example, "She saw them" has no meaning without knowing to which "she" and "them" the sentence refers.

Ambiguous reference: If a pronoun has more than one possible antecedent, change the sentence so that the reference of the pronoun is unmistakably clear. Sometimes the sentence can be made clear by substituting a noun for the pronoun, but in other cases, the sentence must be rewritten. Ambiguous reference can be a particular problem with the pronouns *this, that, these, those, they, them,* and *it*.

> Unclear: After the dogs made muddy footprints on the floors, she was obliged to clean them. (the dogs or the floors?)
> Rephrased: After the dogs made muddy footprints on the floors, she was

obliged to clean the floors.

Unclear: Our sons played with the neighbor's children before they went to their swimming lesson. (who went to the lesson?)

Rephrased: Before our sons went to their swimming lesson, they played with the neighbor's children.

General reference: Avoid using pronouns to refer to general ideas or to replace a series of general statements. General reference can be a particular problem with the pronouns *which*, *this*, *that*, and *it*.

Unclear: Our neighbor allows her cat on the kitchen counters which we disapprove of.

Rephrased: We disapprove of our neighbor's allowing her cat on the kitchen counters.

Unclear: We went to the beach, rented a boat, capsized, and waited the rest of the day for rescue. It was not what I had expected.

Rephrased: We went to the beach, rented a boat, capsized, and waited the rest of the day for rescue. Our day at the beach was not what I had expected.

Unclear: He forgot that the bank would be closed for the holiday. This caused him some difficulty.

Rephrased: He forgot that the bank would be closed for the holiday. This oversight caused him some difficulty.

Since *this* is one of the worst culprits for general reference, a good rule of thumb is to avoid using *this* alone. In other words, use *this* as an adjective (*this* event, *this* idea) rather than as a demonstrative pronoun. See "Demonstrative Pronouns" below.

Demonstrative Pronouns

3.20 When used alone (not modifying a noun), *this*, *that*, *these*, and *those* function as nouns and are considered demonstrative pronouns.

This is a very nice rug.

Those are pretty flowers.

In addition to identifying people or things, the demonstrative pronouns can be used to indicate spatial relationships.

This is my house; *that* is my sister's. (*This* one is nearby; *that* one is farther away.)

Indefinite Pronouns

3.21 An indefinite pronoun does not refer to a specific person or thing. Some common indefinite pronouns are listed below.

all	everybody	no one
another	everyone	one
any	everything	other
anybody	few	several
anyone	many	some
anything	much	somebody
both	most	someone
each	neither	something
each one	nobody	such
either	none	

Indefinite pronouns are often used to make general statements or to indicate quantity.

Everybody knows how upset she was.

Most of the band members showed up for practice.

Unlike personal pronouns, indefinite pronouns use an apostrophe and *s* to form the possessive.

Everyone's cars got muddy after the storm.

He felt that *one's* actions should reflect *one's* beliefs.

Note that if the indefinite pronoun is used as a possessive with *else*, *else* takes the apostrophe and *s*.

No one else's project looked as good as hers.

Personal Pronouns

3.22   A personal pronoun replaces a noun or nouns. The pronoun must always agree in number and gender with the noun or nouns it replaces. Pronouns may be used as subjects or objects in a sentence. When a pronoun is used as the subject in a sentence, the verb must agree with the pronoun in number. Pronouns may also show possession. A possessive pronoun may be used before a noun to show possession (*my* bike), or a possessive pronoun may stand alone. (The bike is *mine*.) See the chart below.

Confusion in pronoun usage frequently occurs with compound subjects or objects (she and I, him and me). The easiest way to determine the correct form of the pronoun is to look at each member of the compound subject or object separately, as in these examples:

Marla and I went home. (*Marla* went home. *I* went home.)

Kim Lee went with him and me. (Kim Lee went with *him*. Kim Lee went with *me*.)

Bruce and he saw the movie. (*Bruce* saw the movie. *He* saw the movie.)

When the compound subject is broken apart in this way, most native speakers will recognize the correct pronoun form.

Note that in the examples above the first person pronouns (I, me; we, us) always appear last in compound subjects and objects.

SINGULAR/ PLURAL	PERSON	NOMINATIVE CASE (SUBJECT)	OBJECTIVE CASE (OBJECT)	POSSESSIVE CASE	
				BEFORE NOUN	STANDING ALONE
singular	first person	I	me	my	mine
singular	second person	you	you	your	yours
singular	third person	he	him	his	his
singular	third person	she	her	her	hers
singular	third person	it	it	its	its
plural	first person	we	us	our	ours
plural	second person	you	you	your	yours
plural	third person	they	them	their	theirs

Confusion may also occur regarding the correct pronoun to use after *than* or *as* (see below). In such constructions, part of the phrase is implied. By completing the phrase, the proper pronoun to use becomes clear.

He runs faster than I. (faster than I do)

She is not as old as he. (as he is)

Sometimes using the correct pronoun is absolutely essential to the meaning of the sentence. Consider the examples below.

He likes frogs better than she. (better than she does)

He likes frogs better than her. (better than he likes her)

Predicate Nominative

3.23   Although "It's me" has become commonly accepted in informal English, it is still not considered proper in formal (especially formal *written*) English. In formal English, the old saying "*Be* takes the nominative" still holds true.

Nominative refers to the "case" of the pronoun. Pronouns take different forms depending on their function in a sentence. These different functions and the forms that correspond to those functions are known as "cases." Subjects are in the nominative case, objects are in the objective case, and nouns and pronouns that show possession are in the possessive case. See "Personal Pronouns," p. 88, for examples of pronouns used as subjects, objects, and possessives.

When a pronoun follows any of the forms of the verb *to be* and refers to the subject, the pronoun is called a predicate nominative and should be in the nominative case (the "subject case").

It was I.

I am she.

It will be he who wins the award.

Pronouns in Incomplete Constructions

3.24   Incomplete constructions are constructions in which some of the words are implied rather than stated. Such constructions occur most frequently after *as* and *than* and often involve a pronoun.

Can he teach her as well as me? (can he teach both of us?)

Can he teach her as well as I? (can he teach as well as I can?)

In the examples above, the meanings of the sentences differ with the pronouns used. To determine which pronoun to use, imagine completing the clause.

He likes frogs better than she. (better than she likes frogs)

He likes frogs better than her. (better than he likes her)

Reflexive and Intensive Pronouns

3.25   Reflexive and intensive pronouns use the same form. They are pronouns that end in *-self* or *-selves*: myself, yourself, herself, himself, itself, ourselves, yourselves, and themselves. They are used to refer to (reflexive) or emphasize (intensive) another noun or pronoun within the sentence.

Reflexive: A reflexive pronoun "reflects" back on an antecedent (the noun or pronoun to which it refers) that is within the same sentence.

> Reflexive: I went by *myself*. (antecedent = I)
>
> Reflexive: We could have done that *ourselves*. (antecedent = we)

Intensive: An intensive pronoun is used to emphasize or intensify an antecedent that is within the same sentence.

> Intensive: The girls *themselves* thought of the idea. (antecedent = the girls)
>
> Intensive: You *yourself* may have seen something similar. (antecedent = you)

Note that both reflexive and intensive pronouns must have an antecedent that is within the same sentence. There is sometimes a tendency to use these pronouns incorrectly in place of personal pronouns.

> Incorrect: She and *myself* went to the store after school. (no antecedent for *myself* in this sentence)
>
> Correct: She and *I* went to the store after school.
>
> Incorrect: He went with *myself*. (no antecedent for *myself* in this sentence)
>
> Correct: He went with *me*.

Relative Pronouns: Who and Whom

3.26   The relative pronouns have different forms depending upon their function in the sentence: subject, object, or possessive.

SUBJECT (Nominative Case)	OBJECT (Objective Case)	POSSESSIVE (Possessive Case)
who	whom	whose
whoever	whomever	whosoever

Confusion often arises over whether to use *who* or *whom*. If the relative pronoun functions as the subject, use who; if it functions as the object, use whom. The difficulty often lies in deciding whether you need a subject or an object.

> Subject: Who is coming for dinner?
>
> Object: Whom are we waiting for?

The easiest way to decide whether to use *who* or *whom* is to mentally drop *who/whom* and the words preceding it and determine whether you can make a sentence with the words that are left by adding *he* or *him*. If you would use *he*, then the sentence needs a subject, and you should use *who*. If you would use *him*, then the sentence needs an object, and you should use *whom*.

> Sentence: Do you know who/whom will be attending the meeting?
>
> Remove who/whom: *will be attending the meeting*
>
> Add he or him: *He* will be attending the meeting.
>
> Correct: Do you know *who* will be attending the meeting?
>
> Sentence: Who/whom is the party for?
>
> Remove who/whom: *is the party for*

Add he or him: Is the party for *him*?

Correct: *Whom* is the party for?

If you are still in doubt whether to use *who* or *whom,* opt for *who.* Using *who* for *whom* may not be correct, but most people won't notice. Using *whom* for *who,* on the other hand, sounds pretentious.

Verbs

Verb Parts

3.27   All verbs have four principal parts: infinitive (sometimes called "plain verb"), present participle, past, and past participle. Present and past participles are used with helping verbs to form verb phrases. Regular verbs form the past and past participle by adding *-d* or *-ed* to the infinitive. Irregular verbs form the past and past participle forms in a different way, such as by changing spelling or by not changing at all.

Regular Verbs

Infinitive	Present Participle	Past	Past Participle
care	caring	cared	cared
call	calling	called	called
jump	jumping	jumped	jumped
walk	walking	walked	walked

Irregular Verbs

Infinitive	Present Participle	Past	Past Participle
become	becoming	became	become
bring	bringing	brought	brought
choose	choosing	chose	chosen
go	going	went	gone
ride	riding	rode	ridden
think	thinking	thought	thought
pay	paying	paid	paid
know	knowing	know	known
shrink	shrinking	shrank (or shrunk)	shrunk (or shrunken)

Verb Phrase

3.28   A verb phrase consists of a main verb and one or more helping verbs (also called auxiliary verbs). A few verb phrases follow:

has gone   is going   will have gone   will be going

Since many verb phrases are formed using the verb *to be*, we review its parts below:

Infinitive	Present Participle	Past	Past Participle
be	being	was, were	been

Tense	Part of Verb Used	Example
present tense	Active: infinitive	Active: I ask.
	(Passive: be + past participle)	(Passive: I am asked.)
present progressive	be + present participle	I am asking.
present emphatic	do + infinitive	I do ask.
present perfect tense	have or has + past participle	I have asked.
present perfect progressive	have or has + be (past participle) + present participle	I have been asking.
past tense	Active: past	Active: I asked.
	(Passive: be [past] and past participle)	(Passive: I was asked.)
past progressive	be (past) + present participle	I was asking.
past emphatic	do (past) + infinitive	I did ask.
past perfect tense	had + past participle	I had asked.
past perfect progressive	had + be (past participle) + present participle	I had been asking.
future tense	Active: will or shall + infinitive	Active: I will ask.
	(Passive: will or shall + be + past participle)	(Passive: I will be asked.)
future progressive	will or shall + be (infinitive) + present participle	I will be asking.
future perfect tense	will (or shall) have + past participle	I will have asked.
future perfect progressive	will (or shall) have + be (past participle) + present participle	I will have been asking.

Verb Tense

3.29   Tense refers to the time element expressed by a verb. Verb tense shows whether an action has already occurred, is now occurring, or will occur in the future. Although there are four principal parts to verbs, these four parts are used to form six tenses: present tense, past tense, future tense, present perfect tense, past perfect tense, and future perfect tense. These tenses can be subdivided into progressive form (*be* + present participle). Present and past can be further subdivided into emphatic. Many of these tenses (progressive, perfect, future, etc.) are formed by verb phrases rather than individual verbs. (See the table on page 93.)

Irregular verb forms are sometimes confused. For example, in the verb *do*, the simple past tense *did* is sometimes incorrectly substituted for the past participle *done* in the perfect tenses. This results in *have did* (wrong) for *have done* (right). The past participles of both *do* and *go* are always used with a helping verb to create the present perfect, the past perfect, and the future perfect tenses.

Simple Past	Perfect tenses used with past participle (shown in italics)		
did	have *done* (not did)	had *done*	will have *done*
went	have *gone* (not went)	had *gone*	will have *gone*

3.30   Sequence of tenses: When a sentence consists of more than one clause, the tense of the main verb affects the tenses of all other verbs

Sequence of Tenses

MAIN VERB	PRESENT				PAST				FUTURE			
	simple present	present progressive	present perfect	present perfect progressive	simple past	past progressive	past perfect	past perfect progressive	simple future	future progressive	future perfect	future perfect progressive
PRESENT TENSE I know because he…	goes home to eat.	is going home to eat.	has gone home to eat.	has been going home to eat.	went home to eat.	was going home to eat.	had gone home to eat.	had been going home to eat.	will go home to eat.	will be going home to eat.	will have gone home to eat.	will have been going home to eat.
PAST TENSE I knew because he…					went home to eat.	was going home to eat.	had gone home to eat.	had been going home to eat.	will go home to eat.	will be going home to eat.	will have gone home to eat.	will have been going home to eat.
FUTURE TENSE I will know because he…	goes home to eat.	is going home to eat.	has gone home to eat.	has been going home to eat.					will go home to eat.	will be going home to eat.	will have gone home to eat.	will have been going home to eat.

in the sentence. The tense of the main verb creates the time frame to which all the other verbs must relate. The tense of other verbs in the sentence should only shift from the tense of the main verb to convey meaning, e.g., to show the order of events.

If the main verb is in present tense, other verbs in the sentence may use any tense. Past or future tense in the main verb, however, imposes time constraints on other verbs in the sentence. For example, if the main verb is in past tense, other verbs in the sentence cannot be in present tense. If the main verb is in future tense, other verbs cannot be in the simple past tense. (See the "Sequence of Tenses" table, p. 93.)

Usage note: There is one exception to the rule that a past tense main verb should not be followed by a present tense verb in a clause. When the clause makes a statement of universal truth, the verb is in the present tense even if the main verb is in the past tense. Consider the examples below.

The teacher *taught* (past) us that a triangle *has* (present) three sides.

We *knew* (past) that he always *goes* (present) home to eat.

3.31 **Special tense problems:** Do not use *would have* in *if* clauses to express the earlier of two past actions. Use the past perfect.

Incorrect: If we would have known, we could have helped.

Correct: If we had known, we could have helped.

Use *would*, not *will*, after a past tense verb.

I *knew* this *would* happen.

Verb Mood

The "mood" of the verb helps to communicate a speaker's attitude. Verbs have three moods: imperative, indicative, and subjunctive. Imperative is used to express commands, warnings, or requests. Indicative is used to express facts or opinions or to ask a question. Subjunctive is used to express a wish or a condition contrary to fact. Subjunctive is also used in *that* clauses that express a suggestion, a demand, or a requirement.

imperative
Go to the store. (command)
I don't think you should *go* to the store. (warning)
Please *go* to the store. (request)

indicative
He *is going* to the store. (statement of fact)
I think he *is going* to the store. (opinion)
Is he *going* to the store? (question)

subjunctive
I wish I *knew* where he was. (wish)
If he *were going* to the store, he could pick up some eggs. (contrary to fact—he is not going to the store)
I suggest that he *be allowed* to go to the store. (suggestion)

> I insist that he *be allowed* to go to the store. (demand)
> It is essential that he *visit* the store. (requirement)

Imperative and indicative moods use the standard verb tenses. Subjunctive, however, has its own rules, as we demonstrate below.

3.32   **Subjunctive mood:** The subjunctive mood is used (1) in *that* clauses to express a demand, suggestion, or request; (2) in sentences with *wish*; and (3) in *if, as if,* or *as though* clauses to express something unlikely or contrary-to-fact. The subjunctive uses *were* or *be* rather than *was* or *is*, and regular verbs do not take an *s* (even with third person singular—he/she) but always use the base infinitive form.

Below, sentences are shown first in present tense subjunctive, then in past tense subjunctive. Note the way in which the verbs change in the subjunctive to show present and past time.

present tense subjunctive

I wish I *knew* the results. (*wish* takes the past tense *[knew]* to show present time)

I insist that she *be seated* by the window. (*be* is used for the verb *to be* in subjunctive *that* clauses)

We demand that she *tell* us the news. (present tense is always used in subjunctive *that* clauses)

I suggest that he *visit* his aunt. (present tense is always used in subjunctive *that* clauses; note that the verb does not take an *s*, even with *he*)

If I *were* in Hawaii, I would go surfing. (*were* shows present time)

Even if he *were* the last man on Earth, she would not go out with him. (*were* shows present time)

past tense subjunctive

I wish I *had known* the results. (*wish* takes the past perfect tense *[had known]* to show past time)

I insisted that she *be seated* by the window. (*insist* changes to past tense to show past time, *that* clause remains the same)

We demanded that she *tell* us the news. (*demand* changes to past tense to show past time, *that* clause remains the same)

I suggested that he *visit* his aunt. (*suggest* changes to past tense to show past time, *that* clause remains the same)

If I *had been* in Hawaii, I would have gone surfing. (past perfect tense shows past time)

Even if he *had been* the last man on Earth, she would not go out with him. (past perfect tense shows past time)

The subjunctive is used with *if, as if,* and *as though* clauses to show that the statement is contrary to fact.

If I *were* the manager, I would do things differently. (The speaker is not the manager.)

When we went on that new space ride, we felt as if we *were* really flying through outer space! (The speaker was not really flying.)

Although the subjunctive may seem unusual, it is in common usage in several everyday expressions: "be that as it may," "suffice it to say," "as it were," "if I were you," and "I wish I knew."

Helping Verbs

3.33   A helping verb (also called an auxiliary verb) is part of a verb phrase. A verb phrase consists of a main verb and a helping verb. Future tense, perfect tense, progressive form, and passive voice are all created using helping verbs.

Verb phrases with the helping verb marked in italics are shown below.

has written   *may* attend   *can* ski   *might have* seen
must read   *will* ride   *shall* go   *would have* taken

Common helping verbs include the following: be, can, could, do, have, may, might, must, shall, should, will, would.

Linking Verbs

3.34   Linking verbs express a state or condition rather than an action. They are called linking verbs because they link the subject to a complement which identifies or describes the subject. This subject complement may be a noun, pronoun, or adjective. Common linking verbs include the following: appear, be, become, feel, grow, look, remain, seem, smell, sound, stay, taste.

Anchovies *taste* salty.

That dog *looks* thin.

She *is* the manager.

Some linking verbs can also be used as action verbs, which can be modified by adverbs. A good way to determine whether the verb is functioning as a linking verb or action verb is to substitute the appropriate forms of *is* and *seem* for the verb. If the sentence still makes sense and has not changed its meaning, then the verb is a linking verb.

Linking verb: He remains happy. (No meaning change—He *is* happy. He *seems* happy.)

Action verb: He remains happily at the park. (Meaning changes; therefore, *remains* is not a linking verb—He *is* happily at the park. He *seems* happily at the park.)

Linking verbs take adjectives. Action verbs take adverbs.

Usage note: *Seem* is always a linking verb. When used as the main verb, *be* is a linking verb except when followed by an adverb. See "Comparing and Contrasting Adjectives and Adverbs," p. 79.

Participle as Verb: Progressive Tense vs. Passive Voice

3.35   The present participle is used with a form of the verb *be* in the progressive tense. The form of *be* determines whether the sentence is present or past progressive.

Progressive = *be* + present participle

Present progressive: The boy is flying a kite.

Past progressive: The boy was flying a kite.

The past participle is used with a form of the verb *be* in passive voice. In passive voice, the subject of the sentence is being acted upon rather than acting.

Passive voice = *be* + past participle

     Passive voice (present): A kite is flown by the boy.

     Passive voice (past): A kite was flown by the boy.

Of course, the past participle is also used with active voice (see examples that follow).

Participle as Verb: Examples of Usage

3.36   Examples of active and passive voice in various tenses follow.

     Active (present): The dog chases the birds.

     Active (present perfect): The dog has chased the birds.

     Active (past): The dog chased the birds.

     Active (past perfect): The dog had chased the birds.

     Active (future): The dog will chase the birds.

     Active (future perfect): The dog will have chased the birds.

     Active (present progressive): The dog is chasing the birds.

     Active (present perfect progressive): The dog has been chasing the birds.

     Active (past progressive): The dog was chasing the birds.

     Active (past perfect progressive): The dog had been chasing the birds.

     Active (future progressive): The dog will be chasing the birds.

     Active (future perfect progressive): The dog will have been chasing the birds.

     Passive (present): The birds are chased by the dog.

     Passive (present perfect): The birds have been chased by the dog.

     Passive (past): The birds were chased by the dog.

     Passive (past perfect): The birds had been chased by the dog.

     Passive (future): The birds will be chased by the dog.

     Passive (future perfect): The birds will have been chased by the dog.

     Passive (present progressive): The birds are being chased by the dog.

     Passive (past progressive): The birds were being chased by the dog.

Verbals

Verbals are formed from verbs, but although they may express action, they do not function as verbs in a sentence. Verbals function as nouns, adjectives, or adverbs. There are three types of verbals: participles, gerunds, and infinitives.

Participle as Verbal

3.37   Participles are present or past participle verb forms that function as adjectives.

     Present participle: I saw the *opening* performance. (adjective)

     Present participle: I saw her *running* toward the house. (adjective)

     Past participle: He was proud of the *completed* project. (adjective)

     Past participle: He repaired the *broken* hinge. (adjective)

Be aware that there can be some confusion when using the term *participle*. In its broadest sense, a participle is any word ending in the suffix -*ing*. In its narrowest sense, a participle is a verb form (which may or may not end in -*ing*) that functions as an adjective. The term *participle* is also used to refer to the verb forms used in the present and past progressive tenses. (See "Verb Parts," p. 91, for more on the present and past participle forms of verbs.)

See "Terminal Participles," p. 109, for more on participles.

Gerund

3.38 A gerund is a verb form ending in -*ing* (present participle) that functions as a noun.

> *Running* is her favorite hobby. (noun)
>
> She likes *skating*. (noun)

The same present participle form of a verb can serve as either a gerund (if it functions as a noun) or as a participle (if it functions as an adjective).

> Gerund: *Practicing* takes discipline. (noun)
>
> Participle: *Practicing*, she played etudes for hours. (adjective)

Infinitive

3.39 The infinitive form of a verb can be used as a noun, an adjective, or an adverb. Infinitives are usually preceded by *to,* although not always.

> We like *to ski*. (noun)
>
> She left the party *to take* a nap. (adverb)
>
> On the chair are clothes *to iron*. (adjective)

Be careful not to confuse the *to* that is part of the infinitive with the *to* used as a preposition. The infinitive is *to* + verb. The preposition is *to* + noun (or pronoun).

> infinitive: We are going *to shop*.
>
> preposition: We are going *to the store*.

3.40 **Split infinitives:** Splitting an infinitive means putting one or more words between *to* and the verb—e.g., to boldly go. In some cases, a strong argument can be made in favor of splitting the infinitive to promote readability (to *more than* double production). When splitting the infinitive helps readability, it is becoming increasingly acceptable to allow the split. Let functionality be your guide. If readability is not significantly improved by splitting the infinitive then don't.

> Split infinitive: The professor asked me *to* carefully *grade* the papers. (infinitive = to grade)
>
> Corrected: The professor asked me *to grade* the papers carefully.
>
> Split infinitive: The teacher asked him *to* independently *work* on the project. (infinitive = to work)
>
> Corrected: The teacher asked him *to work* independently on the project.
>
> Split infinitive: It was her first time on ice skates, and she wanted *to* slowly *go* around the rink. (infinitive = to go)

Corrected: It was her first time on ice skates, and she wanted *to go* around the rink slowly.

Parts of a Sentence

Clauses

Clauses are groups of words that work together in a sentence. Clauses may function as nouns, adjectives, or adverbs in a sentence. All clauses contain both a subject and a predicate. There are other groups of words that work together in sentences, but unless these word groups contain both a subject and a predicate, they are not considered clauses. Grammarians refer to "nonclauses" as phrases (see "Phrases," p. 101). Phrases may contain a subject or a verb but not both.

Clause: as the store closed

Phrase: at the store

Clause: we went home

Phrase: going home

Clauses are classified into two main categories depending on whether or not they make sense standing alone: (1) clauses that make sense standing alone are called independent, or main, clauses and (2) clauses that do not make sense standing alone are called dependent, or subordinate, clauses.

Independent Clause/Main Clause

3.41   The terms *independent clause* and *main clause* can be used interchangeably. Independent clauses make sense standing alone. An independent clause is a group of words that represent a complete thought and contain a subject and verb. Adding an initial capital and ending punctuation transforms an independent clause into a simple sentence. Many sentences consist of nothing but an independent clause; however, a sentence may also contain one or more dependent clauses and even additional independent clauses.

Independent clause: it was a hot, humid day

Independent clause: I needed a cool drink

Two simple sentences: It was a hot, humid day. I needed a cool drink.

Note that by definition an independent clause is not a sentence. To be used as a sentence, an independent clause must begin with a capital letter and end with an appropriate punctuation mark.

Dependent Clause/Subordinate Clause

3.42   The terms *dependent clause* and *subordinate clause* can be used interchangeably. A subordinate clause does not represent a complete thought and cannot stand alone.

Dependent clause: where my brother had gone

Dependent clause: whom he was seeing

Dependent clauses must be combined with independent clauses in order to form sentences. In the sentences below, *we knew* and *we wondered* are independent clauses.

> Simple sentence: We knew *where my brother had gone.*

> Simple sentence: We wondered *whom he was seeing.*

For information on punctuating sentences containing independent and dependent clauses, see "Clauses and Punctuation," p. 121.

Distinguishing Between Dependent and Independent Clauses

3.43   Distinguishing between dependent and independent clauses is not as difficult as it may first appear.

> Independent clause: he had a cat

> Dependent clause: before he had a cat

> Independent clause: I ran the race

> Dependent clause: while I ran the race

> Independent clause: the car stalls

> Dependent clause: if the car stalls

The trick is to look at the first word in the clause. The clause is independent unless it begins with a subordinating conjunction or a relative pronoun.

subordinating conjunctions
after, although, as, as if, as much as, as though, because, before, even though, how, if, in order that, inasmuch as, provided, since, so that, than, that, though, unless, until, when, whenever, where, wherever, whether, which, while, who, whom, whose

relative pronouns
that, what, whatever, which, whichever, who, whoever, whom, whomever, whose, whosoever

To aid in spotting subordinating conjunctions, it is helpful to know that subordinating conjunctions are the only words in English that always begin clauses. In other words, subordinating conjunctions are always the first word in a clause (never the second word, third word, etc.). This tip is particularly helpful because there is another group of words that is sometimes confused with subordinating conjunctions: conjunctive adverbs.

conjunctive adverbs
accordingly, also, anyhow, anyway, as a result, besides, consequently, finally, first, for example, for instance, furthermore, hence, however, in addition, in conclusion, in fact, incidentally, indeed, instead, later, likewise, moreover, namely, nevertheless, on the contrary, otherwise, second, still, that is, therefore, to be sure, too

Like subordinating conjunctions, conjunctive adverbs act as transitional devices in sentences. Unlike subordinating conjunctions, however, conjunctive adverbs are the most movable of words in English. Also, conjunctive adverbs do not begin clauses. Consider the examples below.

> However, we know what to do.   We know, however, what to do.

> We know what to do, however.

In the first example above, it may appear that the conjunctive adverb *however* begins a subordinate clause, but notice in the second two examples that *however* is not actually part of the clause at all. *However* can function equally well at the beginning, middle, or end of a sentence. Use this test of movability to aid in distinguishing subordinating conjunctions from conjunctive adverbs.

(See "Subordinating Conjunctions," p. 84, "Relative Pronouns: Who and Whom," p. 90, and "Semicolon," p. 120 for more information.)

Phrases

In casual conversation, *phrase* refers to any group of words that function together. In the study of English, however, *phrase* has a more specific meaning, and we distinguish between phrases and clauses (see "Clauses," p. 99). All groups of words that function together are either clauses (which contain both a subject and a verb) or nonclauses (which do not contain both a subject and a verb); nonclauses are phrases. So a phrase is a group of words that act as a unit and contain either a subject or a verb but not both.

Phrases may function as nouns, verbs, or modifiers. Phrases may be located anywhere in a sentence, but when they begin a sentence, they are usually followed by a comma. Like dependent clauses, phrases cannot stand alone. If a phrase is not part of a complete sentence, it is a sentence fragment.

Walking to the park was fun. (phrase functioning as a noun)

The dog *was running* quickly. (phrase functioning as a verb)

That is the prettiest flower *in the garden*. (phrase functioning as an adjective—modifies flower)

We went *to the mall*. (phrase functioning as an adverb—modifies went)

Phrases tend to be confused with dependent clauses because neither of them forms a complete thought. Remember, a clause will have both a subject and a verb. A phrase will have one or the other but not both.

Absolute Phrase

3.44 The absolute phrase, or nominative absolute, is grammatically independent from the rest of the sentence. (In this case, "absolute" means independent or freewheeling.) The absolute phrase functions as a modifier without modifying any specific element in a sentence. The absolute phrase consists of a noun (or pronoun) followed by a participle. Absolute phrases may fall in any position in a sentence.

The plans having been made, we went into the kitchen for coffee.

The boy remembered her, *her hair blowing in the wind*.

I followed the trail, *the dog leading the way*, until I came to the cabin.

USAGE   Agreement

Agreement: Noun with Plural Possessive Pronoun

4.1   The nouns that follow plural possessive pronouns may be singular or plural. Plural possessive pronouns used in a collective sense are followed by singular nouns; plural possessive pronouns used in a plural sense are followed by plural nouns.

> Collective: My neighbors brought *their dog*. (more than one person, one dog)
>
> Plural: The children brought *their dogs*. (more than one child, more than one dog)
>
> Collective: We pushed *our car* to get it started. (more than one person, one car)
>
> Plural: We moved *our chairs* closer to the fire. (more than one person, more than one chair)

When the noun following a plural possessive pronoun represents something abstract or figurative, the noun is frequently singular even when the pronoun is meant to have a plural sense.

> Concrete noun: The council members took *their seats*.
>
> Abstract noun: The council members maintained *their dignity* during the proceedings.
>
> Concrete noun: The skaters laced *their skates*.
>
> Figurative noun: The skaters waited for *their moment* on the ice.

See also Usage note under "Agreement: Pronoun with Antecedent," below.

Agreement: Pronoun with Antecedent

4.2   A pronoun must agree with its antecedent in number and gender. The antecedent is the noun or noun phrase to which the pronoun refers.

> Sentence: *The kittens* chased the mouse. (replace *the kittens* with a pronoun)
>
> Plural antecedent—plural pronoun: *They* chased the mouse.
>
> Sentence: *The boy* flew a kite. (replace *the boy* with a pronoun)
>
> Singular, masculine antecedent—singular, masculine pronoun: *He* flew a kite.

Be especially careful to make a possessive pronoun agree with its antecedent.

> Correct: An artist is admired for her skill with a brush.
>
> Incorrect: An artist is admired for their skill with a brush.

Usage note: The growing trend of using *their* to mean *his* or *her* has served to add confusion to the rules of agreement in number. When *their* is used incorrectly to mean *his* or *her,* it is frequently followed by a singular noun, as in the example below.

> A teacher is responsible for *their classroom*.

We hear the construction above more frequently in conversation than the use of *their* as a plural possessive. This leads the ear to expect *their* to be followed by a singular noun. (See also Usage Note with "Agreement: Pronoun with Antecedent.")

Use *who* (or *that*) to refer to people and *which* (or *that*) to refer to objects. Either *who* or *which* can be used to refer to animals, depending on whether the animal is personified.

Incorrect: People which talk during movies annoy me.

Correct: People who talk during movies annoy me.

Correct: People that talk during movies annoy me.

Incorrect: The book who he is reading is a mystery novel.

Correct: The book that he is reading is a mystery novel.

Correct: The dog that runs through our yard is a nuisance.

Correct: Our dog, who never misses an opportunity to play, grabbed the towel I was using.

Correct: The cat which sat on the hearth looked quite content.

Agreement: Verb with Subject (Noun)

4.3   A subject and verb agree if they are both singular or both plural, that is, the subject and verb must agree in number.

Nouns are singular when they refer to one person, place, or thing and plural when they refer to more than one (cat—singular, cats—plural).

Most verbs ending in *s* are singular, while verbs not ending in *s* are plural. The exception to this general rule is verbs used with *I* and singular *you* (which takes the same verb form as plural *you*). Although *I* and *you* are singular, their verbs do not take an *s*: I go, you go, he goes, it goes, they go, we go.

The number of the subject is not affected by any phrases that fall between the subject and the verb. (See "Agreement: Verb with Indefinite Pronoun," p. 105, for the only exception.)

Sentence: The difficulties of going on a long trip were apparent.

Subject: the difficulties (plural)

Verb: were (plural)

The verb should agree with the subject, even when the subject and predicate are inverted.

Performing for the first time on this stage are the Lowell sisters. (subject = Lowell sisters, plural verb = are)

Performing for the first time on this stage is Winifred Lowell. (subject = Winifred Lowell, singular verb = is)

Agreement: Verb with Collective Subject

4.4   Collective nouns refer to groups: army, audience, band, chorus, class, clergy, club, committee, community, council, couple, crew, crowd, faculty, family, flock, fruit, gang, government, group, herd, jury, league, membership, mass, orchestra, pack, platoon, police, press, public, quartet, squad, staff, swarm, team, troop, varsity, etc.

A collective noun may take either a singular or plural verb depending on how the noun is used. If a collective noun is used to refer to a group as a whole, it will take a singular verb. If it refers to the members of a group, a plural verb is used.

Singular sense: The audience was restless.

Plural sense: The committee have been arguing among themselves.

Agreement: Pronoun with Collective Subject

4.5   A collective noun may take either a singular or a plural pronoun depending on how the noun is used.

Singular sense: The team announced its victory.

Plural sense: The class improved their scores.

Singular sense: Use all of your head.

Plural sense: Use all ten of your fingers.

Agreement: Verb with Compound Subject

4.6   Compound subjects are formed by joining words or groups of words with *and, or,* or *nor*.

Subjects joined with *and* take a plural verb. This rule is true whether the words making up the compound subject are singular or plural.

Single subject: Our cat spends a lot of time in the back yard.

Compound subject: Our cat and dog spend a lot of time in the back yard.

Compound subject: Our cats and dogs spend a lot of time in the back yard.

Compound subject: Our cat and dogs spend a lot of time in the back yard.

Compound subject: Our cats and dog spend a lot of time in the back yard.

Note that sometimes *and* is used as part of a phrase that functions as a unit to name a single item. In these cases, the subject is not a compound subject.

Example: Macaroni and cheese is my favorite dish.

Example: Stop and Go was the name of the market.

Singular subjects joined with *or* or *nor* take a singular verb.

Example: A chair or a stool fits under the counter.

Example: Either our cat or our dog sits on the couch.

Example: Neither Melissa nor Jody plays the clarinet.

When plural subjects are joined with *or* or *nor*, they take a plural verb.

Example: Jackets or sweaters are needed in the evenings.

Example: Either his parents or my parents take us to the pool.

Example: Neither our cats nor our dogs like to have baths.

When one or more plural subjects are joined to one or more singular subjects with *or* or *nor*, make the verb agree with the closer of the two subjects.

Example: A sports coat or evening clothes are required for the dinner party.

Example: Evening clothes or a sports coat is required for the dinner party.

Example: Either my parents or my aunt drives us to school.

Example: Either my aunt or my parents drive us to school.

Example: Neither the secretaries nor the supervisor was happy about the arrangement.

Example: Neither the supervisor nor the secretaries were happy about the arrangement.

Agreement: Personal Pronoun with Compound Subject

4.7 Compound subjects joined with *and* take plural pronouns.
> Bryan and Ian took their dogs on a walk.

Compound subjects joined with *or* or *nor* take singular pronouns.
> Neither Bryan nor Ian took his dog on a walk.

Difficulties can develop when the nouns in a compound subject joined with *or* or *nor* are of different genders.
> Neither Bryan nor Lisa took his or her dog on a walk.

See "Agreement: Possessive Personal Pronoun with Indefinite Pronoun," below, for a discussion of gender issues with pronouns.

Agreement: Verb with Indefinite Pronoun

4.8   The verb must agree with the indefinite pronoun in number. Some of the indefinite pronouns take singular verbs, others take plural verbs, and others vary depending on context.

Singular: another, anybody, anyone, anything, each, each one, either, everybody, everyone, everything, much, neither, nobody, no one, one, other, somebody, someone, something
> Everybody has a car.   Each of the parents has a car.

Plural: both, few, many, several
> Both students have cars.   Several students have cars.

Vary (sometimes singular, sometimes plural): all, any, most, none, some
> Most of the cars were dirty.   Most of the car was dirty.

Note that the indefinite pronouns that can be either singular or plural *(all, any, most, none, some)* constitute an exception to the standard rule of agreement that the number of the subject is not affected by any phrases that fall between the subject and the verb. When *all, any, most, none,* or *some* refer to a singular noun, they take a singular verb. When they refer to a plural noun, they take a plural verb.
> Singular: *Some* of the paper *is* dry.
> Plural: *Some* of the papers *are* on the desk.

Agreement: Possessive Personal Pronoun with Indefinite Pronoun

4.9   When indefinite pronouns serve as antecedents for pronouns, the personal pronoun must agree in number with the indefinite pronoun: singular indefinite pronouns take singular personal pronouns, plural indefinite pronouns take plural personal pronouns (see lists of singular and plural indefinite pronouns in "Agreement: Verb with Indefinite Pronouns," above).

Plural: *Some* have their own cars.

Singular: *Each* has his or her own.

Agreement with indefinite pronouns does not sound difficult in theory, but agreement with the singular indefinite pronouns has become rather troublesome in practice because of the issue of gender. Indefinite pronouns do not reflect gender, but personal pronouns do. Consider the example that follows.

Everybody in class brought his lunch on "bag day."

If everyone in class is not male, we may prefer the construction below.

Everybody in class brought his or her lunch on "bag day."

Although accurate and grammatically correct, the construction above is awkward. Frequently, the resolution to this dilemma in spoken English is to use a plural personal pronoun as shown below.

Everybody in class brought their lunch on "bag day."

There may come a time when using *their* to mean *his or her* is acceptable in standard English, but currently, such usage is still considered incorrect. The best solution in many cases may be to reword the sentence—use a noun rather than an indefinite pronoun.

The students in class brought their lunches on "bag day."

Agreement: Adjective with Noun/Pronoun

4.10   An adjective and the noun or pronoun it modifies must agree in number.

She has *two* brothers.

Give me a piece. (articles *a* and *an* are adjectives)

When *this, that, these,* and *those* are used as adjectives, they must agree in number with the noun or pronoun that they are modifying.

Singular: *this* bird, *that* alligator, *this* kind

Plural: *these* sparrows, *those* crocodiles, *these* kinds

Clarity

Grammatical structure and punctuation can enhance communication or, if used improperly, obscure meaning. See "Pronouns—Clear Reference," p. 86, and "Comma—To Avoid Ambiguity," p. 115.

Parallel Structure

4.11   A sentence is parallel when equal or closely related ideas are expressed by grammatical elements of equal rank (nouns paired with nouns, phrases paired with phrases, clauses paired with clauses, etc.). Parallel structure adds clarity, smoothness, and polish to writing. There are three situations in which parallel construction should always be used: (1) constructions using coordinating conjunctions, (2) constructions using correlative conjunctions, and (3) constructions comparing or contrasting elements.

Coordinating Constructions

4.12   When two or more ideas are joined by a coordinating conjunction (for, and, nor, but, or, yet, so), each of the ideas should be in the same grammatical form (part of speech).

> Not parallel: The dog was *short*, *fat*, and *had a lot of hair*. (two adjectives and a verb phrase)
>
> Parallel: The dog was *short*, *fat*, and *hairy*. (all adjectives)
>
> Not parallel: We went *sailing* and *on a picnic*. (gerund and prepositional phrase)
>
> Parallel: We went *sailing* and *picnicking*. (two gerunds)
>
> Not Parallel: Cost is how much is paid, and payback is how much people are getting.
>
> Parallel: Cost is how much is paid, and payback is how much is received.

See "Coordinating Conjunctions," p. 82, for more information.

Correlative Constructions

4.13   The correlative conjunctions (both...and, either...or, not only...but also, etc.) should join grammatical elements of equal weight.

> Not parallel: The cat was both *finicky* and *did not obey well*. (adjective and verb phrase)
>
> Parallel: The cat was both *finicky* and *disobedient*. (two adjectives)

See "Correlative Conjunctions," p. 83, for more information.

Comparing and Contrasting Constructions

4.14   When two or more ideas are compared or contrasted, each idea should be the same part of speech.

> Not parallel: *Basketball* no longer interests me as much as *to watch soccer*. (noun and infinitive)
>
> Parallel: *Basketball* no longer interests me as much as *soccer*. (two nouns)
>
> Parallel: *To watch basketball* no longer interests me as much as *to watch soccer*. (two infinitives)
>
> Not parallel: He is known more for his *showmanship* than for *what he has done in athletics*. (noun and clause)
>
> Parallel: He is known more for his *showmanship* than for his *athleticism*. (two nouns)
>
> Not parallel: *Playing* ball is more fun than *to do* homework. (gerund and infinitive)
>
> Parallel: *Playing* ball is more fun than *doing* homework. (two gerunds)

Problems with Modifiers

Improper use or placement of modifiers can cause confusion for readers. This confusion can range from momentary uncertainty about the writer's meaning to inability to discern the writer's meaning at all. However, modifiers gone astray can also add humor to the serious business of English grammar, as in the examples below.

> Riding my new mountain bike, the neighbor's dog chased me down the street.
>
> The man basted the chicken wearing an apron.

Misplaced Modifiers

4.15   Modifiers describe, define, clarify, or provide more explicit information about the words they modify. There is nothing intrinsic to the modifiers themselves that shows which word they modify; therefore, modifiers must be carefully placed in sentences so that it is clear which words they modify. Modifiers are said to be misplaced when it is unclear which word they modify or when they modify the wrong word. In general, modifiers should be placed as close as possible to the words they modify. Frequently, misplaced modifiers can be corrected simply by moving the ambiguous phrase closer to the word it modifies.

> Misplaced: I spoke with the woman who is standing by the potted palm in the yellow dress.

In the example above, the reader may think that the palm is draped in a yellow dress. Correct this confusion by relocating the modifier.

> Corrected: I spoke with the woman in the yellow dress who is standing by the potted palm.

Now there is no confusion over who is wearing the yellow dress. In the example below, there is some confusion over who is in the back of the truck.

> Misplaced: He took the dog when he left this morning in the back of the truck.
>
> Corrected: When he left this morning, he took the dog in the back of the truck.

Now it is clear who is riding in the back of the truck.

Dangling Modifiers

4.16   Dangling modifiers occur when a modifying phrase or clause does not clearly modify a word in the sentence or seems to clearly modify a word other than the one the writer intended. A dangling modifier usually appears at the beginning of a sentence, and the word that it should be modifying either is not in the sentence or is not the grammatical subject (as opposed to the implied subject) of the sentence. When a modifier dangles, the actual, literal meaning of the sentence is far different from the meaning the writer intended.

Introductory participial phrases are common culprits for dangling and are referred to as dangling participles.

> Dangling: Walking across the parking lot, her purse strap broke.
>
> Corrected: Walking across the parking lot, she felt her purse strap break.
>
> Corrected: While she was walking across the parking lot, her purse strap broke.

In the first example shown, the introductory participial phrase modifies "her purse strap." Since her purse strap could not possibly have been walking across the parking lot, the sentence must be rephrased so that either the noun that the participial phrase is modifying follows it directly or the participial phrase is changed to an adverb clause. Below is another example of a dangling participle.

> Dangling: Newly renovated, we enjoyed traveling the road. (phrase modifies the subject *we*)
>
> Corrected: We enjoyed traveling the newly renovated road.

It is not just participial phrases, however, that can dangle. Other introductory phrases can also be left dangling when the grammatical subject of the sentence is not the word that the phrase is intended to modify.

> Dangling: By leaving early for the concert, good seats were assured. (phrase modifies the subject *seats*)
>
> Corrected: By leaving early for the concert, we assured ourselves of good seats.
>
> Dangling: Alone in the building, the wind rattling the windows terrified her. (phrase modifies the subject *wind*)
>
> Corrected: Alone in the building, she was terrified by the wind rattling the windows.
>
> Dangling: After jogging a mile, a drink of water was all I wanted. (phrase modifies the subject *drink*)
>
> Corrected: After jogging a mile, all I wanted was a drink of water.
>
> Dangling: While swimming in the pool, my neighbor was seen pruning her roses. (phrase modifies the subject *neighbor*)
>
> Corrected: While swimming in the pool, I saw my neighbor pruning her roses.
>
> Dangling: To explore the Grand Canyon, a hike to the bottom is recommended. (phrase modifies the subject *hike*)
>
> Corrected: To explore the Grand Canyon, you should hike to the bottom.

The easiest way to deal with dangling modifiers is to figure out what word the phrase should be modifying and then make sure that word is the grammatical subject of the sentence.

Terminal Participles

4.17   Participial phrases are such useful modifiers that there is a tendency to use them where they don't belong. Participial phrases are always adjectives and like all adjectives they must modify a noun or pronoun. Adjectives cannot modify phrases or clauses. When a participial phrase is used at the end of a sentence (terminal participle), the phrase must modify either the noun just preceding it or the subject of the sentence. In the examples below, note the use of the comma to show whether the participial phrase is with the word it modifies (no comma) or is removed from that word (comma).

> He ran the course *zigzagging up the hill*. (modifies *course*)
>
> He ran the course, *singing as he went*. (modifies *he*)

Participial phrases cannot be used to modify concepts. In the first two sentences below, the terminal participle was intended to modify the concept of running rivers. In actuality, however, the participial phrase modifies either the noun directly preceding it (as in the first example below) or the subject (as in the second example). The corrected example states the intended meaning.

> Incorrect: He was running rivers in a kayak *adding adventure to his life.* (modifies *kayak*)

> Incorrect: He was running rivers in a kayak, *adding adventure to his life.* (modifies *he*)

> Correct: Running rivers in a kayak added adventure to his life.

Special (Confused) Word Pairs/Incorrect Word for Context

4.18   In this level of *Editor in Chief®*, we focus on the following confused pairs of words:

> affect (most commonly used as a verb meaning "to influence"; in psychology may also be used as a noun meaning "emotion") / effect (most commonly used as a noun meaning "the result"; may also be used as a verb meaning "to cause")

> affective (emotional) / effective (having an intended result)

> among (used with collective quantities: argument among members) / between (used with distinct quantities: argument between Bob, Joan, and Ned)

> anxious (uneasy, apprehensive) / eager (earnestly desiring something)

> are (form of verb to be) / our (possessive of first person plural)

> as (used when followed by a verb: "We left at 1:00 as planned.") / like (used when followed by a noun: "The boy ran like the wind.")

> bring (to carry something with oneself to a place—from here to there—when you bring something with you, you arrive with it) / take (carry to another place—from here to there—when you take something with you, you leave with it)

> can (to be able to) / may (to be permitted to—used when asking for permission)

> consideration (careful thought) / consolation (comfort, solace)

> disinterested (impartial) / uninterested (indifferent)

> endurable (bearable) / enduring (lasting)

> eminent (standing out) / imminent (about to happen)

> farther (used to refer to physical distance: "5 miles farther") / further (used to refer to abstract distance: "to gain further understanding")

> fewer or few (used with countable plural nouns: "9 items or fewer") / less or little (used with singular nouns not easily counted: "less rain than expected")

> imply (to suggest without stating directly) / infer (derive a conclusion)

> inhabit (live in) / inhibit (suppress or hold back)

> lay (transitive verb meaning to put or place) / lie (intransitive verb meaning to rest or recline)

Note: for information on "could care less," see CONTENT, p. 81.

Unnecessary Words

4.19   Unnecessary words should be deleted.

Negatives: Use only one negative word to state a negative idea.

> Incorrect: We don't have no bananas.

Correct: We don't have any bananas.

Correct: We have no bananas.

The words *hardly* and *scarcely* are also considered negative words and should not be used with other negatives.

Incorrect: We have hardly no bananas.

Correct: We have hardly any bananas.

Correct: We have no bananas.

Some words are excessive or repetitive and should be deleted.

Incorrect: The thing is is the people are hungry.

Correct: The people are hungry. (or The thing is, the people are hungry.)

Incorrect: Rover he ran away.

Correct: Rover ran away. (or He ran away.)

Incorrect: We are, like, hungry!

Correct: We are hungry!

Subject: Use a noun or pronoun (not both) as subject.

Incorrect: Marnie she had a lovely coat.

Correct: Marnie had a lovely coat.

Correct: She had a lovely coat.

PUNCTUATION

Apostrophe

5.1 Use an apostrophe in contractions to show where letters or numbers have been left out.

could not = couldn't   let us = let's   it is = it's
the 1990s = the '90s

Note that *its* (without apostrophe) is the possessive form of *it*. (See Homonyms, p. 123.)

5.2 Use an apostrophe to form the plural of letters, but do not use an apostrophe to form the plural of numbers.

Mind your p's and q's.

Shakespeare lived in the late 1500s and early 1600s.

Usage note: At one time, forming the plural of numbers by adding apostrophe *s* was common; however, in current style manuals, the preference is to drop the apostrophe. If you wish to use an apostrophe when forming plural numbers, note that under no circumstances is the construction '90's considered correct.

5.3 Use an apostrophe to form the possessive, not the plural, of a word.

5.4 Add *'s* to form the singular possessive. (An exception is the possessive form of *it*—see Apostrophe [5.1], above.)

dog's bone   Maria's ball   car's color
one year's time   brother-in-law's family   the water's edge

5.5 Add an apostrophe to form the possessive of a plural ending in *-s*, *-es*, or *-ies*.

cats' toys   foxes' holes   butterflies' flowers

board of directors' meeting   five cents' worth   two weeks' vacation

parentheses' location   analyses' results

5.6   Add *'s* to form the possessive of plural nouns that do not end in *s*.

women's hats   sheep's wool   children's toys   tomorrow's news

bacteria's virulence   feet's position   phenomena's occurrence

5.7   Add *'s* to form the possessive of indefinite pronouns.

anyone's idea   everybody's school   someone's gloves   someone else's love

Usage note: Possessive pronouns do not use an apostrophe to form the possessive. See "Pronouns," p. 86.

Apostrophes are unnecessary with the regular plurals of words (*the parents of the boys*).

Colon

5.8   Use a colon between numbers indicating hours and minutes.

We will arrive at 9:15.

5.9   A colon follows the greeting in a business letter.

Dear Sir: Dear Dr. Martinez:

5.10   Use a colon to introduce a list of items.

We needed three things at the market: milk, flour, and eggs.

5.11   Use a colon with *as follows* and *the following* when the example immediately follows.

He gave us the following example of a typical fall Saturday in the yard: rake the leaves, mow the lawn, and enjoy a cold drink in the lounge chair.

5.12   Use a colon to introduce a clause or phrase that explains, restates, illustrates, or provides more information about the preceding clause.

He was always unique: the only time he wore matching socks was on "clash day."

The last hope of many endangered species may be zoo breeding programs: captive breeding of endangered animals that are then released into the wild.

5.13   Usage note: Style manuals recommend that an independent clause precede a colon and that a colon not fall between a verb and its objects.

Incorrect: His backpack contained: books, binders, and his lunch.

Correct: His backpack contained books, binders, and his lunch.

Correct: His backpack contained the following: books, binders, and his lunch.

Correct: His backpack contained three types of items: books, binders, and his lunch.

5.14   The colon always falls outside quotation marks or parentheses.

We went to see "Taming of the Shrew": it is my favorite play.

While preparing for the expedition, they told us to beware of the following (if we still wanted to go after reading the list): poisonous snakes, malarial mosquitoes, parasitic worms, dysentery amoeba.

Comma

Conventional Uses

5.15   Use a comma to separate the elements of an address (street and city, city and state), but do not use a comma to separate the ZIP code.

5 Elm Street, Sample Town, New York   Monterey, CA 93940

5.16   Use a comma after the state in a sentence when using the format city, state.

We are going to Sample Town, New York, to visit our grandmother.

5.17   Use a comma in dates between day and year in the format month, day, year.

January 10, 1996   April 5, 2001

Usage note: If you follow the European model, write 9 May 1999—
no commas.

5.18   Use a comma after the year in a sentence when using the format month, day, year.

We have to be in Nevada on January 10, 1996, in order to visit our friends.

5.19   Use a comma after the greeting of a friendly letter.

Dear Emilio,

Usage note: Business letters use a colon after the salutation.

5.20   Use a comma to separate a name and title when the title immediately follows the name.

Randall Brown, Principal   Lois Gonzalez, Manager

5.21   Use a comma after the closing of a letter.

Sincerely,   With best wishes,   Love,

Items in a Series

5.22   Use a comma between words or phrases in a series.

blue, red, and green   up the hill, over the log, and down the hole

Usage note: Some sources may consider the comma before *and* optional. For the purpose of consistency in this series, include the comma before *and*.

5.23   Commas are sometimes used between short, parallel independent clauses.

We came, we saw, we ate.

Mom went to dinner, Dad played golf, and I stayed home.

Usage note: Commas are not used between independent clauses that are neither short nor parallel when the clauses are not separated by coordinating conjunctions. This error is known as comma splice or comma fault. See "Semicolon," p. 120, for more information.

5.24   Use a comma to separate coordinate adjectives (adjectives that equally modify a noun).

She had a warm, friendly smile.

Usage note: See "Coordinate and Noncoordinate Modifiers," p. 79, for more information.

Introductory Elements

5.25 Use a comma to separate an introductory word or interjection from the rest of the sentence.

Yes, I have heard of that TV show.   Hey, did you see that comet?

Well, I guess that's true.

5.26 Use commas to set off an introductory phrase or dependent clause that precedes a main clause unless the introductory phrase or clause immediately precedes the main verb.

After we left, she phoned the office.

From the couch, the cat jumped onto the bookcase.

On the water lay a fifty-foot schooner.

Usage note: Dependent clauses are also referred to as subordinate clauses. See "Subordinating Conjunctions," p. 84, for more information.

Interrupters/Nonessential Elements

5.27 Use commas to separate nouns of address from the rest of the sentence.

Kim, I asked you to step over here.

You know, Rebecca, we could go to the store tomorrow.

5.28 Use commas to set off sentence interrupters.

The recent game, on the other hand, showed the wisdom of working on plays.

He had told us, however, that he would study more.

5.29 Set off nonessential appositives (a noun or noun/pronoun phrase next to a noun, which identifies, defines, or explains the noun) with commas.

The tomato, or "love apple," was first cultivated in Central America.

The Marsdens, our nearest neighbors, left on vacation today.

My brother's dog, the big white one, is rolling in the leaves.

Her oldest brother, Jim, is leaving for college tomorrow.

5.30 Usage note: There is often confusion about when to set off people's names or the titles of books, movies, etc. with commas. If the name or title specifies which person, book, etc. is being referred to, then it is essential to the meaning of the sentence and should not be set off with commas. In the last example above, we have already specified that her "oldest brother" is leaving for college. His name is not essential to the meaning of the sentence (since she can only have one oldest brother) and so we set off his name with commas. Consider these examples.

Her brother, Jim, is leaving for college tomorrow. (She only has one brother, so the name is not essential to the meaning of the sentence.)

Her brother Jim is leaving for college tomorrow. (She has more than one brother, and it is Jim who is leaving tomorrow. Jim's name specifies which brother is leaving and is, therefore, essential to the meaning of the sentence.)

5.31 Set off nonessential (nonrestrictive) phrases or clauses with commas.

The dog, who always had a mind of his own, started shedding in January.

Usage note: See "Clauses and Punctuation," p. 121, for more information.

5.32 Use commas to set off absolute phrases.

She stared at the gray water, her face set in harsh lines.

The day fading into dusk, he took his leave.

Usage note: See "Absolute Phrase," p. 101, for more information on absolute phrases.

5.33 Use commas to set off modifying phrases that do not immediately precede the word or phrase they modify; for example, in the first sentence below, *the* falls between the modifiers and the noun they modify.

Old and venerable, the oak had stood for 75 years.

I stuffed the family cats, both highly vocal about their predicament, into the cat carrier.

5.34 Use commas to set off contrasting expressions within a sentence.

She turned 27, not 25, on her last birthday.

He likes jazz, not rock and roll.

5.35 Use a comma to introduce a direct question.

He wanted to ask, Where are you from?

The question is, Does he really want the job?

To avoid ambiguity or misreading

5.36 I stayed with my brother, and my sister and my aunt went skiing.

Sally spoke to Ruth, and Tom spoke to George.

I told Mary, Jane was missing.

What I say I will do, I do.

He stood against the wall, towering over his friends.

See also "Terminal Participles," p. 109.

With Conjunctions

5.37 Use commas before coordinating conjunctions joining two independent clauses.

We took the bus, but she will take the train.

My sister mowed the lawn, and I raked the leaves.

Usage note: See "Conjunctions," p. 82, for more information.

5.38 Use a comma after a conjunctive adverb.

I don't like what you say; however, I support your right right to say it.

(See also "Conjunctive Adverbs," p. 100.)

With Quotation Marks

5.39 Use a comma to separate a direct quote from a phrase identifying the speaker.

> Tomas said, "We had fun doing English today."
>
> "We had fun doing English today," Tomas said.
>
> "Go to the third rock," the game manual read. (virtual "speaker" in this case)

5.40 Place commas inside ending quotation marks.

> The package was marked "fragile," but the contents were quite sturdy.
>
> "We had fun doing English today," Tomas said.

Usage note: We have noted some confusion over this particular rule, possibly because British usage differs from American usage. American style manuals, however, are all in agreement: commas and periods always go inside closing quotation marks. There is an interesting story about this punctuation style. It is said that when typesetting began in America, the lead used to make the type was not as refined as that used in England, and the printers had problems with the small commas and periods outside the quotation marks breaking off. To solve this problem, they moved the commas and periods inside the quotation marks! In American punctuation, the periods and commas go inside the quotation marks while the larger colons and semicolons go outside the quotation marks.

When *Not* to Use Commas

5.41 Commas are sometimes used inappropriately. Below are some of the more common errors in comma usage. No comma should be used

a between the month and year in a sentence
> Incorrect: We will visit Georgia in July, 1996.

b when all items in a series are joined by *or* or *and*
> Incorrect (delete both commas): We went sledding, and skating, and skiing.
> Incorrect (delete both commas): I don't know Gerard, or Manuel, or Alan.

c with noncoordinate adjectives
> Incorrect: I saw a big, orange cat under the porch.

d after a dependent phrase or clause just before the main verb
> Incorrect: On the floor, lay a bat.

e between a subject and its verb
> Incorrect: The chairman of the arts, told the committee to vote.

f before a subordinating conjunction (dependent clause/main clause)
> Incorrect: He ran into the house, because it started raining.

g to separate adjectives and adverbs joined by *but*
> Incorrect: a car with plush, but costly upholstery
> Incorrect: he fell, reaching for a branch but missing

h   with a compound predicate
         Incorrect: The barking dog chased the mailman, and bit him.

i   with an essential clause, phrase, or appositive
         Incorrect: The manager quit, because she was planning to move.
         Incorrect: He mowed the yard, in exchange for a meal.
         Incorrect: The American, Rita, is coming. (unless there is only one American)

j   to separate adverbs or an adverb phrase
         Incorrect: He turned the knob left, and right.
         Incorrect (delete 2nd comma): None of them won, although, they were all good.

k   to separate a dependent clause
         Incorrect: The room was filled with chairs used so often, that they were rickety.

l   when dependent clause follows main clause
         Incorrect: He will see us, if he comes.

m   to separate compound objects
         Incorrect: Lift your arms, and legs.

n   between two independent clauses not separated by a coordinating conjunction (see Run-on Sentences and Comma Splice," p. 123).

o   between dependent clauses
         Incorrect: She thinks that she is ugly, and that they dislike her.

(See also "Clauses and Punctuation," p. 121.)

Exclamation Point

5.42   Use an exclamation point after an exclamatory sentence.
          Stop that dog!   We know what to do!   I love chocolate!

5.43   Use an exclamation point after an interjection that stands alone.
          Stop! Don't you know to look both ways before crossing a street?

          Usage note: An interjection that begins a sentence may function as an introductory word and be set off from the sentence with a comma instead of an exclamation point; for example, Hey, wait for me!

5.44   Place the exclamation point inside quotation marks at the end of a quoted exclamation.
          Incorrect: "Get that snake off the counter"! screamed Jamie.
          Correct: "Get that snake off the counter!" screamed Jamie.

5.45   Usage note: In contrast to commas and periods (which always fall inside closing quotation marks), an exclamation point falls inside closing quotation marks only when it applies to what is inside the quotation marks. If it is not part of the quoted material, it goes outside the quotation marks; for example, That box is marked "fragile"!

5.46   Place the exclamation point within closing parentheses when the exclamation point applies to the word, phrase, or clause within the parentheses. When the exclamation point applies to the sentence rather than the parenthetical material, it falls outside the closing parenthesis.

> In our house, Thanksgiving lasts two weeks. (Great, Mom, turkey goulash, how original!)

> It took us three days to requisition the materials (one day for shipping and two days to fill out forms!).

> Ronald gave a flawless performance (if you ignored the minor slip-ups)!

Usage note: Unlike periods and question marks, which have standard usage, use of exclamation points is at the discretion of the writer. In the examples above, the positions of the exclamation points show what the writer wished to emphasize.

Hyphen

5.47 Use a hyphen with compound numbers.
> twenty-five   ninety-four   forty-three

5.48 Use a hyphen to create temporary compound adjectives (unit modifiers). See "Compound Adjectives," p. 80.
> half-baked plan   six-year-old boy   much-loved doll

Parentheses

5.49 Use parentheses (in pairs) to enclose "parenthetic information" (phrases and clauses that add information or explanations).
> My favorite exhibit at the aquarium was the sea otters (*Enhydra lutris*).

5.50 If an entire sentence is enclosed within parentheses, then the period should also fall within the parentheses. However, if the parentheses enclose an independent clause that is part of a longer sentence, the independent clause should not end in a period.
> My neighbor got a new cat. (She already has three others.)

> My neighbor's new cat (she already has three others) is orange.

5.51 A question mark or exclamation point may be used with a parenthetic element that is part of a longer sentence.
> My aunt (poor woman!) is now supporting her son and his three children.

> After waiting in line for two hours to get advance tickets, we found (who could have known?) that there was no line at all at the gate and plenty of tickets remaining.

Period

5.52 Use a period to end a declarative sentence. See also "Run-on Sentences," p. 123.
> A sentence begins with a capital letter and ends with a punctuation mark.

5.53 Use a period after abbreviations and initials.
> Washington, D.C.   Dr. Nolan   Mr. J. Pedrewski

Usage Note: It is becoming more acceptable to use some common abbreviations without periods, e.g., mph, km, etc. However, for the purposes of consistency in this series, use the periods with abbreviations.

5.54 Always place periods inside closing quotation marks.

We delivered a package marked "fragile."

See usage note under "Comma."

5.55 A period falls within closing parentheses only if the entire sentence is within the parentheses. If the parentheses enclose material that is part of a longer sentence, the period (or other punctuation ending the sentence) falls outside the parentheses.

He said that the dog ate the liver off his plate (he didn't say how the dog got the liver in the first place).

The physics professor used humor to enliven his lectures. (In fact, we suspected that he really wanted to be a comedian.)

Question Mark

5.56 Use a question mark after a direct question (interrogative sentence).

Are we there yet?   What time is it?

5.57 Do not use a question mark with a statement or indirect question.

I wondered if I could do that.   We asked him how he liked the play.

5.58 Place a question mark inside the quotation marks after a quoted question.

"What day is soccer practice?" asked Lucia.

5.59 Usage note: Again in contrast to commas and periods (which always fall inside closing quotation marks), a question mark falls inside closing quotation marks only when it applies to what is inside the quotation marks. In the following example, the question mark applies to the entire sentence, not to the word inside the quotation marks: Is that box marked "fragile"?

Quotation Marks, Double

5.60 Use quotation marks to enclose direct quotes (include both parts of a divided quotation).

"I need help on this English paper," said Grover.

"This beautiful day," said Mark, "is too good to waste indoors."

5.61 Do not use quotation marks with indirect quotes.

He said that it was a beautiful day.

5.62 When a direct quote is longer than one paragraph, place quotation marks only at the beginning of each paragraph and at the end of the last paragraph. (The following example is quoted from *The Story of English* by McCrum, Cran, and MacNeil.)

"Shakespeare is universal in his appeal and sympathy not least because he wrote in a language that has become global....

"He was a country boy, born in Stratford, in the heart of Warwickshire, then a town of some 1500 inhabitants."

5.63 Use quotation marks on the titles of songs, stories, poems, articles, book chapters, or television shows.

We have to memorize "Jabberwocky" by Thursday.

5.64 Use quotation marks to set off unusual words/phrases or words/phrases used in unusual ways.

She had a "punny" sense of humor.

He was a "dinner at eight" kind of guy.

Quotation Marks, Single

5.65 Single quotation marks are used to enclose a quotation within a quotation.

"I always thought his 'poor me' attitude was an act," Eugenie said.

5.66 When single and double quotation marks appear together, punctuation that normally would fall within the double quotation marks should fall within both the single and double quotation marks.

Heather said, "Before the game, our coach told us 'United we stand; divided we fall.'"

5.67 Usage note: The rules for usage of other punctuation (e.g., period, comma) with quotation marks apply to single quotation marks as well as to double quotation marks.

Semicolon

5.68 A semicolon is used between closely related independent clauses that are not joined by a coordinating conjunction.

The dog dreamed on the porch; the neighbor's cat slipped quietly along the porch rail.

5.69 Use a semicolon between independent clauses joined by conjunctive adverbs. Adverbs that serve as conjunctions include accordingly, also, anyhow, anyway, besides, consequently, finally, first, furthermore, hence, however, incidentally, indeed, instead, later, likewise, moreover, namely, nevertheless, otherwise, second, still, that is, therefore, and too. Some prepositional phrases and infinitives also function as conjunctive adverbs: as a result, for example, for instance, in addition, in conclusion, in fact, on the contrary, to be sure.

She always had a strong sense of style; in fact, she became a highly regarded decorator.

5.70 Use semicolons to separate items in a series when the items themselves use commas.

The team consisted of both national and international players: Peter Schmeichel, goal keeper, Denmark; Ryan Giggs, left wing, Wales; Steve Bruce, center back and captain, England.

5.71 Semicolons fall outside parentheses.

We wanted to go on an exotic vacation (at least I did); however, the only vacation spot we could afford was Disney World.

5.72   Semicolons fall outside quotation marks.

She had said the place was really "original"; I wasn't expecting black lights and purple walls.

See also "Run-On Sentences," p. 123.

Multiple Punctuation

5.73   In general, two marks of punctuation should not be used together except in the cases of brackets, parentheses, quotation marks, ellipses, and dashes.

Incorrect: What was her expression when you said, "I know you did it."?

Correct: What was her expression when you said, "I know you did it"?

Clauses and Punctuation

Recognizing dependent and independent clauses is useful when one is punctuating sentences. In some instances, commas are required between dependent and independent clauses, and in other cases, they are not. Following are a few simple rules of thumb for when to use commas in sentences containing clauses:

5.74   independent clause + independent clause =

comma after the first clause when the clauses are joined by a coordinating conjunction

Example: The sun was shining brightly, and the weather was warm.

5.75   independent clause + independent clause =

semicolon after the first clause when the clauses are not joined by a coordinating conjunction

Example: The sun was shining brightly; the weather was warm.

5.76   dependent clause + independent clause =

comma after the dependent clause

Example: After we left for the country, the package we were waiting for arrived.

5.77   independent clause + dependent clause =

usually no comma, however, this varies depending on whether the dependent clause is restrictive (essential) or nonrestrictive (nonessential)

5.78   independent clause + dependent clause (when dependent clause immediately precedes main verb) =

no comma

Example: Only after we had studied did we take the test.

5.79   (independent clause +) dependent clause + dependent clause =

no comma

Example: He knows that he is smart and that he is handsome.

For more on the difference between restrictive (essential) and nonrestrictive (nonessential) see "Essential vs. Nonessential," below.

To aid in remembering some general rules for punctuating

clauses, think of them as follows:

    I + I = comma or semicolon

    I + D = no comma

    D + I = comma

Note that the rules above apply to clauses, not phrases. For more on the difference between clauses and phrases, see pages 99-101.

See "Comma," p. 113, and "Semicolon," p. 120, for more information on punctuating clauses.

Essential vs. Nonessential

5.80   Restrictive (essential) clauses or phrases are essential to the meaning of the sentence. Removing them would change the meaning of the sentence. Nonrestrictive (nonessential) clauses or phrases can be removed without altering the meaning of the sentence; they give additional or incidental information which is not essential to the basic idea that the sentence is conveying.

> Nonrestrictive (nonessential): Our neighbor, who is sitting in that chair by the wall, is well-liked in our community.

> Restrictive (essential): The man who is sitting in that chair by the wall is our neighbor.

Consider the difference in meaning of the two examples below.

> Nonrestrictive (nonessential): The girl, who is wearing a very odd hat, stood indecisively before the classroom door.

> Restrictive (essential): The girl who is wearing a very odd hat stood indecisively before the classroom door.

In the first example above, the girl who is the subject of the sentence is the only girl standing in front of the door, and we are given incidental information about her. In the second example, there are other girls standing in front of the door, and we are given information to help us identify to which girl the sentence refers.

To test a phrase or clause to see whether it is essential or nonessential, imagine that the commas are handles that you can use to lift the phrase or clause out of the sentence. If the basic meaning of the sentence does not change, then the phrase or clause is nonessential and should be set off with commas. If the basic meaning of the sentence changes, then the phrase or clause is essential and should not be set off with commas.

The general punctuation trend is toward using fewer commas, and this trend is noticeable with nonessential clauses. In cases where nonessential clauses do not seem obviously parenthetical, the clauses are increasingly not set off with commas. For example, nonessential clauses beginning with *while* or *whereas* frequently do not take commas unless the clauses are long. In the examples below, both punctuation patterns shown for the nonessential clause will be commonly seen.

> Essential: She finally ate her dinner while the baby was sleeping.

Nonessential: She likes coffee while her friend prefers tea.

Nonessential: She likes coffee, while her friend prefers tea.

As a rule of thumb, commas are usually used with nonessential clauses beginning with *who*, *which*, *where*, or *when*.

Run-on Sentences and Comma Splices

5.81   Run-on sentences and comma splices may be corrected by using a semicolon, conjunction (coordinating or subordinating), or colon or by creating two sentences. In this level of *Editor in Chief*®, the answer key shows the best answers based on the context; however, there may be acceptable answers that are not shown.

Incorrect (run on): Bob played his harp he was rehearsing for tonight's performance.

Incorrect (comma splice): Bob played his harp, he was rehearsing for tonight's performance.

Correct: Bob played his harp. He was rehearsing for tonight's performance.

Correct: Bob played his harp; he was rehearsing for tonight's performance.

Correct: Bob played his harp: he was rehearsing for tonight's performance.

Correct: Bob played his harp because he was rehearsing for tonight's performance.

Sentence Fragments

5.82   In this level of *Editor in Chief*®, the answer key corrects sentence fragments by joining the sentence fragment to a complete sentence.

Incorrect: The bird was sitting on the roof. Sunning himself.

Correct: The bird was sitting on the roof, sunning himself.

Note that a sentence fragment may also be corrected by rewriting the sentence in other ways, as shown below.

Possible: Sunning himself, the bird sat on the roof.

SPELLING

Homonyms

6.1   In this level of *Editor in Chief*®, we focus on the following homonyms:

hear/here	sole/soul	to/too/two
its/it's	stationary/stationery	whose/who's
principal/principle	their/they're/there	your/you're

Note: some words that sound similar are listed under "Special (Confused) Word Pairs/Incorrect Word for Context," p. 110.

Plurals

6.2   Some words have the same form for the singular and plural.

sheep   deer

6.3   The plurals of words that end in the sound of *f* are usually formed by changing the *f* to *v* and adding *-es*. There are, however, exceptions.

   leaf/leaves   knife/knives   roof/roofs

6.4   The plurals of words that end in *y* are usually formed by changing the *y* to *i* and adding *-es*.

   berry/berries   carry/carries

6.5   Some nouns have unusual plural spellings (e.g., *es* replaces *is*, *a* replaces *on*)

   analysis/analyses   criterion/criteria   phenomenon/phenomena

Possessives

See "Apostrophe," p. 111.

Closed and Open Spellings

6.6   In general, verb phrases consisting of a verb + preposition are open (two words, no hyphen). The same two words are combined when functioning as a noun.

   clean up: verb phrase / cleanup: noun

   pick up: verb phrase / pickup: noun

Other open/closed spellings follow:

   care less: verb phrase / careless: adjective

   a lot: a lot is always two words (never alot)

   all right: unlike already (all ready), all right is always two words (never alright)

   in to/into

Miscellaneous Spellings

6.7   The following miscellaneous spelling words appear in errored form in this edition of *Editor in Chief*®:

   bursting   manufacturers
   can you   separately
   coral   through